CLOUGH
MAXWELL
& ME

CLOUGH
MAXWELL
& ME

EXPLOSIVE, THE INSIDE TRACK
STUART WEBB

north
bridge.co.uk
PUBLISHING

First published in Great Britain in 2016 by

North Bridge Publishing
20 Chain Lane
Mickleover
Derby DE3 9AJ

© Stuart Webb, 2016

The right of Stuart Webb to be identified as the Author of this work has been asserted by him in accordance with the Copyright, Designs and Patents Act 1988

All rights reserved. No part of this book may be printed, reproduced or utilized in any form or by any electronic, mechanical or other means, now known or hereafter invented, including photocopying and recording, or in any information storage retrieval system, without permission in writing from the publishers

ISBN 978-0-9954517-0-4

Printed and bound by Jellyfish Solutions, Swansmore, Hampshire

Visit the North Bridge Publishing website for our other local books on Derby
www.northbridgepublishing.co.uk
or search on Amazon for North Bridge Publishing

amazon.com

Contents

Acknowledgements 9
Foreword 11
Shooting Stars 17
Press Gang 32
Jumping the Gun. 41
Title and Tantrums 54
You Can't Win 'Em All, Brian 71
Mackay to the Rescue 88
Champions Again 99
A Colourful Cast .109
Thrill of the Chase 120
A Strange Appointment. 129
Cloughie's Big Stitch Up 137
Doc's Quick Fix. .146
Judgment Day 158
Captain Bob. 172
Bouncing Czechs. 187
The Name's Cox, Arthur Cox 204
Lionel, Jim and Another Promotion. . . .216
My All Star Rams Team 235
Money Ball 243
No Regrets 250

Dedication

To my wife, Josie – our wedding was the most significant and fortunate event of my life – and to the wonderful supporters who have followed the Rams throughout all the ups and downs and without whom there would be no Derby County.

Acknowledgements

THERE are a number of people I want to thank for their help in putting together this book.

The contribution of Mirror Group sports writers Will Price and Tom Hopkinson has been amazing. Their assistance and commitment in keeping me focused and in helping me put all my stories and memories on to paper has proved invaluable.

I thank Alan Hinton for his eloquent Foreword, which paves the way for the reader to step behind the scenes and into the corridors of the Baseball Ground during such critical and successful times in the Rams history.

I am also grateful to Arthur Willis (alas no longer with us), Geoff Glossop, Barrie Eccleston and Don Shaw for sharing their own personal memories of those exciting, eventful and turbulent days of Clough, Maxwell and Me.

Foreword
by Alan Hinton
(Derby County and England)

I FIRST met Stuart Webb in the late spring of 1970. A sharp dresser with an even sharper mind, Stuart arrived at the Baseball Ground as the Rams' new secretary, and in the years that followed, if he did wonderfully well in business then he did even better on behalf of Derby County Football Club.

Here was a man who certainly possessed an entrepreneurial spirit. Crucially, he also had inner steel. He certainly needed it, given the aggravation that came his way when he acted as the buffer between Brian Clough and the Derby directors. Stuart was verbally punched from pillar to post in keeping open the lines of communication between the two parties. He dealt with it in great style and with supreme diplomacy.

Cloughie seemed to be against Stuart almost from the off. Which was remarkable because it was Brian who had brought him in from Preston North End in the first place. But then, as everyone knows, Cloughie had to control everyone and everything. Most of the board didn't have a clue about how to cope with Brian. But Stuart handled him beautifully, which the manager obviously didn't like. In the dressing room, behind Stuart's back, he'd often dish out the most fearful abuse. Yet when I visited Stuart on one of my recent trips back to England from Seattle, and I asked him why he never used the arsenal of ammunition he had against Clough – "Why didn't you ever challenge Brian and tell him you had some stuff on him, so he would back off?" – Stuart replied: "Because that would have been wrong. It wasn't about my feelings. It was about making Derby County the best club in the land." Sheer class.

Soon after my arrival at the club from Nottingham Forest in 1967, I worked out that if Cloughie was having a go at you, the best move was to be nice as pie in return. Then he tended to lose interest and selected another target. Brian could be a bully, but he was a winner who knew how to motivate the players found by Peter Taylor, the master talent spotter.

I stuck up for Stuart on many occasions against the manager because I always stick up for what is right in my eyes. Sometimes I stood up for him against my own teammates, some of whom were envious because he'd branched out from the Baseball Ground to create the extremely successful Lonsdale Travel business with his wife, Josie. I told them: "No one is stopping you doing something similar – no one."

None of those guys ever complained when we flew to and from European matches by private plane, one of the many perks that Stuart could arrange for us through Lonsdale. Luxury travel made us feel special – like we deserved to mix it with the very best.

FOREWORD

Maybe Stuart would have been a better 'fit' at a more glamorous club – Manchester United, for example, or one of the big London outfits, Chelsea or Tottenham maybe – but be sure of one thing: it was a lucky day for Derby County when Stuart Webb agreed to join the Rams.

Now he has written this book. As well as tales of their run-ins, Stuart has some fantastic stories about how he, Brian and Peter signed some of the lads I played with. Fortunately for the sake of the club – and their own sanity – Brian and Stuart *could* work brilliantly well together, notably when they hit on a plan to sell season tickets for two years in advance. That scheme generated a cash windfall as supporters responded enthusiastically, lapping up the idea to the benefit of Brian's transfer kitty. Yes, when the two of them worked in tandem, Derby County prospered and grew.

When trouble brewed, Brian always had the team onside because he put us together and he was a brilliant manager, although he would never have achieved what he did without Peter's help. Peter constantly tried to get 'a bit of this and a bit of that' from Stuart for the players. He was always on the lookout to improve our lot in all sorts of ways.

Both men knew Stuart was their route to the club coffers so they either put pressure on him to plead their case to the board, or alternatively ranted and raved at him when the board said 'no'. Pressure? The weight of it must have been enormous at times. But I admired and respected Stuart because he was coolness personified, never allowing the players to see that he was feeling that pressure, even in the most frantic of moments. And there were plenty of those.

Was Stuart's reaction important? Yes, it was. To be at their most successful, footballers need no distractions. Had they detected fear or panic in Stuart's eyes, rather than calm authority, you can bet that whispers and rumours would have spread throughout our tight-knit group.

The two biggest episodes in Stuart's time at Derby County saw Brian and Peter depart, and, 11 years later, the club saved from extinction. From the best team in England and a European Cup semi-final, to attendances of 10,000, life in the Third Division, and going out of business altogether in little more than a decade. What a fall from grace for one of the 12 founder members of the Football League. Scandalous.

If Cloughie's resignation sparked chaos, it began to subside only because Stuart recruited Dave Mackay as his replacement. Stuart knew Dave was the best man for the job, perhaps the only man, because he was already a Derby legend from his playing days.

And don't forget: Clough wasn't sacked – he *resigned*. And he should never have done that. Much as all the players respected the manager and everything he did for us as a group and individually, that resignation letter he dictated did not contain the savviest words Brian ever uttered.

I had long since left Derby and was in Vancouver during the club's battle to stay in existence in their centenary year. If no one but Dave Mackay could have worked in the hot seat in 1973, and won the First Division title two years later, then no one but Stuart Webb could have done the business in 1984. He steered the club through the darkest of days, pleading virtually on bended knee in the High Court to keep the club afloat. Derby

FOREWORD

County supporters, like me, owe him a massive debt of gratitude for that.

On a personal level, Stuart was brilliant during my playing days. His advice and guidance, not forgetting Derby's amazing supporters, helped make my testimonial match against a Great Britain XI in 1976 a huge success. He was especially good when my wife, Joy, and I lost our son, Matthew, at the age of nine. Stuart was there all the way for us during an incredibly difficult period in our lives. I will never forget that and I am delighted to claim him as a good and loyal friend.

We enjoyed wonderful days at Derby County, everyone involved with the club in our era will tell you that. Stuart was there a lot longer than most of us in a succession of absolutely key roles behind the scenes. I've heard plenty of Stuart's tales – shocking, humorous and enlightening – from a lifetime in football and for ages I've been encouraging him to commit them to a book. Now he has.

His stories about Brian Clough, Robert Maxwell, Arthur Cox, Jim Smith and other larger-than-life characters will have you roaring with laughter and shaking your head in disbelief, I'm sure. I am confident that you will find this a hugely enjoyable and very amusing read. And I guarantee you will discover other sides to men you thought you knew so well.

My very best wishes to Stuart Webb, and to all Derby County fans, wherever you are in the world.

1

Shooting Stars

MAJOR POWERS in the First Division twitched in the autumn of 1969 as Brian Clough drove his Derby County upstarts to beat Tottenham Hotspur 5-0, then Liverpool 4-0. Soon he was trying to ride roughshod over the Football Association and the Football League as well. The Rams were like something out of the Wild West. Cloughie was Billy the Kid, Peter Taylor was riding shotgun. There was a bumpy road ahead.

The manager made a scene out of introducing me to the club as secretary yet, within months, two incidents involving money left us wary of each other. When people ask about my relationship with Brian, I answer: "What relationship? It never got started." There were weeks when we would pass each other in the cramped corridors of the Baseball Ground and he chose to pointedly ignore me. He wasn't so much difficult, or challenging to work with, as impossible sometimes.

Let's be clear: he was a football genius in terms of success on the pitch, an exceptional manager, and he could be utterly charming, noble and generous – a true gentleman when he chose to be and someone you'd think you would like to cherish as a friend. He was a humanitarian, he was a politician, he supported the striking miners and dished out FA Cup-tie tickets to those manning the picket lines while our fans were queuing round the ground. As for charisma, he had it by the bucketload.

No wonder the Derby fans idolised him. Who could blame them? He made some inspired signings to mould a team capable of producing fabulous, winning football. Results meant they loved him with a passion. He was extremely successful, great for Derby, a hero. I learned to watch my feet, as well as my back, as the Baseball Ground corridors became cluttered by bunches of flowers, baskets of fruit, bottles of champagne and crates of booze brought in by fans and admirers. It was as if someone was preparing for an expedition.

It's just that some of the other stuff that went into making Brian Howard Clough such a Machiavellian character wasn't so endearing.

* * * * *

I see matches on TV, played in magnificent, state-of-the-art, all-seater stadiums such as the Emirates at Arsenal, and wonder if those supporters get as much enjoyment out of watching the game as I did as a youngster at Deepdale. When I close my eyes, I count my blessings at how vividly I can still recall being passed down to the front of the packed terraces and gently lifted over the top of a small whitewashed wall to sit on the cinder track – close enough to reach out and touch my hero the Preston Plumber, Tom Finney, who was the Lionel Messi of his day. On a cold winter's afternoon in the gathering gloom before the floodlights came on for the second half, I was transfixed, staring across the pitch to where it seemed as if a thousand fireflies were dancing as the half-time cigarettes were lit in the wooden old West Stand – so much for health and safety.

My mum, Irene, and dad, Wilfred, who was the town clerk for Fylde Rural District Council, brought me up with a strong work ethic, although I also found time to enjoy playing as an amateur on the books of Morecambe and Fleetwood Town, then both non-League clubs. I liked the "playmaker" role, wearing the number-10 shirt – or the inside-left as it was known in those days. I left Preston's Harris College, now the University of Central Lancashire, in 1958 at the age of 17 to join Titus, Thorp & Ainsworth, a prestigious firm of accountants whose offices in Winckley Square were opposite those of the Football League in the days before the League upped sticks and moved to Lytham St Annes.

Titus, Thorp & Ainsworth sound as if they could be a handy trio of half-backs and it just so happened that they scrutinised the books of several professional clubs as well as the Football League. It almost felt like my destiny to go into the game. Just as I was on the point of taking my articles to become a chartered accountant in 1961, I was tipped the wink that Preston North End were looking for an assistant to the secretary, George Haworth, and that's how I got my job there.

The year 1964 was a huge one for me, both professionally and personally. May saw George, me and two part-time lads, both of whom worked on the railway, dealing with a flood of ticket applications as Preston reached the FA Cup Final. And what a day out it was for us all beneath the famous Twin Towers, especially our teenage right-half Howard Kendall who, at 17 years 245 days, became the youngest player to appear in a Wembley Cup Final. Our luck was out, though, and West Ham United beat us 3-2.

July brought a red-letter day when Josie, who I had courted since our college days, did me the great honour of agreeing to become my lovely wife. It was the most significant and fortunate event of my life.

They were super days at North End, which became an unofficial feeder club for Bill Shankly's Liverpool. The great man had played for Preston and found his way back to Deepdale on a regular basis to take Gordon Milne, Peter Thompson and Dave Wilson to Anfield. But both Shanks and Sir Matt Busby at Manchester United woke up too late to the enormous talents of Kendall, who went off to seek his fame and fortune under Harry Catterick at Everton.

* * * * *

In April 1970, I was 28 and doing well as assistant secretary, yet feeling that I might have outgrown Preston, when a telephone call came from Peter Taylor. Derby County were looking for a new club secretary. Would I be prepared to come down and see Brian? Brian's other right-hand man at Derby, Jimmy Gordon, who had previously coached at nearby Blackburn Rovers, had mentioned to the Rams management that I was developing a reputation as a bit of a whiz kid. Stoke City and Tottenham

Hotspur had already approached me but I was being groomed for the top job at Preston, a well-respected, balanced club even if a downturn in fortunes meant they had recently been relegated to the Third Division. Still, there would be no harm in listening to what Mr Clough had to say. No pressure to take the job, if it was offered to me. Or so I thought.

A few days later I drove with Josie and our baby daughter, Beverley, through the Peak District to look around Derby to see if we liked the place, but really thinking that we'd just have a cup of tea and a chat with Brian before going home. I had work at Deepdale the following day.

We headed towards the town's main railway station to meet Brian at the Midland Hotel, his stomping ground. He was king of the Midland. It was all very relaxed, chatting over afternoon tea, civil and nicely done. Brian explained that the club needed somebody to come in because they had huge problems with their administration. Their sudden success — Baseball Ground attendances now sometimes touched 40,000 where, two years earlier, 20,000 would have been a good gate — had overwhelmed them. After a joint FA-Football League enquiry Derby had just been fined £10,000, not to mention being banned from playing in any form of European football for 12 months. Derby's mayor had called it "a terrible injustice". It was certainly a mess. Brian told me that I came highly recommended. Would I fancy sorting it out?

Before I could reply, Brian clapped his hands, jumped from his chair and gave me a glimpse of the force of his personality. It was like someone flicking on an electric switch. "Right, we've agreed, you're going to stay overnight," he stated.

"I can't do that," I protested. "I've got to get back."

"No, no. It will all be done in the morning: Baseball Ground, 9.30 sharp. Don't be late."

I said we'd got no change of clothes with us, or anything else for that matter. "Leave all that to me, young man. I'll organise everything," and he did, summoning Bill Wainwright, the hotel's general manager. Shaving tackle and pyjamas for me, a stylish nightdress for Josie, and toys for Beverley duly appeared in our complimentary suite.

I was up in good time, and as the football ground was only a short drive from the Midland Hotel, through those tight, terraced streets so typical of where Victorian football bosses had built their stadiums – right among where the supporters lived and worked in factories that were still belching smoke 100 years later – I expected to be in and out, meeting the chairman and perhaps one or two directors, and back home in Preston for lunchtime.

I arrived at the Baseball Ground to be greeted by an array of expensive cars, including Rolls-Royces. Inside the ground, where a full board meeting was in session, there was an expectant hum all around the place. In those days it was unusual to find a football ground "alive" in the middle of the week. But Derby County's home was certainly buzzing.

I walked the corridors looking for Brian, asking staff where I might find him, when he popped up like a genie from a bottle, dressed for training. He looked me up and down as if I was on military parade, smiled and said: "Ready? Come on, meet the directors." Brian knocked on the boardroom door and walked in without waiting for a response. That smile widened into a broad beam as he pushed me forward, announcing: "Mr Chairman, directors. This is the man I want to be the new secretary of Derby County Football Club. Look after him, Mr Chairman, won't you? And, oh, by the way, gentlemen, I have to go now, some of us have work to do, so I'll leave you to it." In his trademark drawl, he added for emphasis: "I've got to look after the most important people in this club – the players."

I stood there like an idiot, a little boy in front of the headmaster, while the men facing me looked around, mouths gaping. Sensing the embarrassment, the chairman, Sydney Bradley, stood up and said: "Excuse me, gentlemen," as he bustled me out of the room. Outside, Bradley wasted no time in saying: "We'd like to offer you the job because Brian wants you." They didn't know me from Adam, didn't ask what plans or innovations I might have. The very fact Brian wanted me was enough for them. I had been inside the club for only two minutes and here was an indication of the power Brian wielded. The men who thought they were running the club were actually in thrall to him.

Back at Preston that afternoon, my boss was less than impressed with my timekeeping, and I was embarrassed for the second time that day, explaining I'd been to see some people in the East Midlands and that they wanted to give me a job. Written terms soon arrived from Derby, offering me a salary of £2,500 a year plus a car. It wasn't big time, but Josie and I felt it was a good step up, and I was intrigued by the prospect of working with Brian and his assistant, Peter Taylor. Josie, like everybody, was quite taken by Brian's style.

The Preston directors were shocked by developments. I had been there eight years. My boss George Haworth was 60, a bit of an old-stager, almost ready for retirement, and the new blood on the board wanted me to stay and take his job. However, Josie and I had made up our minds that we were going to move. I served a short notice period and came to Derby, ready to begin at the Baseball Ground on Monday, 1 June 1970 … 9.30am sharp, just as Brian had reminded me.

I had barely got my feet under the table when, on Tuesday, 2 June, an office girl came in to tell me: "There's a policeman to see you, Mr Webb." "Welcome to Derby!" I thought. Maybe I'd parked illegally. I was relieved, yet perplexed, when a uniformed officer asked politely: "Can I talk to you about my son, Michael Dunford? He's been working here as an office junior, but he's been sent home by Brian Clough. My wife's upset, I'm upset, and we were hoping that you could do something about it."

I promised to investigate and told Mr Dunford that I would get back to him. I didn't have a clue what had gone on but I knew I had to find out, and quickly. It didn't take long to discover that, while I was occupied elsewhere on my first day, Brian had seized the opportunity to march up to Michael and demand: "Where are the keys to the safe?" Michael, quite correctly, refused to hand them over … only to be sent home by the manager on the spot. It sounded dramatic and I let it be known that I would be talking to the chairman, Sam Longson, who had taken over from Sydney Bradley, returning to the post for a second term. I needed to seek his advice on a case of what appeared to be bullying and unfair dismissal.

Brian was seething as he insisted: "It's nothing to do with the chairman, I'm running the club." Clough versus Webb. Round one. That's how it all started.

Sam had been on holiday when I was appointed, and was initially put out that an important decision had been taken without his say-so. He was also keen to wash his hands of the affair involving the Dunfords and snapped: "Look, you sort it out. You're the new administration. You wanted the job. Ball's in your court, Stuart."

Against Brian's better wishes, of course, I duly reinstated Michael Dunford who later became my assistant and had a long and distinguished career in football serving the Rams, Everton, Birmingham City and Plymouth Argyle. Meanwhile, I tried to identify clearly defined boundaries that I hoped would enable the manager and myself to work together for the good of the club. I wanted nothing to do with the football side of things. Why would I dream of interfering with coaching? That was not my remit. I had no expertise in that quarter. However, company law dictated that, as secretary, I was in charge of administrative matters; I was legally responsible for the club's finances. If I was coming in, that's what I was going to do. That was my territory, along with seeking sponsorship and other commercial ideas that I successfully implemented.

Derby County had to be squeaky clean following the inspection carried out by the Football League's accountant and his assistant which led to that fine and cruelly denied Dave Mackay and Co the opportunity to compete in the 1970-71 European Fairs Cup against clubs such as Juventus, Inter Milan, Barcelona and Bayern Munich. European friendlies were also off limits for a year.

Shambles sums up the entire episode – from the chaos unearthed by the probe to the manner in which the result was conveyed to the Baseball Ground. It's impossible to know whether the club was selected at random for a book inspection, as was claimed at the time, or whether a "little bird" had been chirping about things behind the scenes at Derby not being quite right. Brian Clough was a big noise now and there were those who would delight in him being muffled and taken down a peg or two.

The fact remained that Derby had an appalling crime sheet. No club in their history had paid more in fines. You could go back to 1941 when a Rams manager and several directors were suspended and the club secretary severely censured for offences that had occurred before the war. In 1949 the chairman and secretary were suspended after all sorts of offences including withholding money from the Inland Revenue. Never a good move! Quite clearly, it was not a business that endeared itself to the authorities. This time eight offences were proven, adding up to a conviction for "gross negligence", although the joint Football Association and Football League commission reported that "there was no question of any fraud or dishonesty against any person now or formerly connected with the club".

Chief among the offences was a failure to lodge new contracts for Les Green, Frank Wignall and John Richardson. Then there were the payments for, and continued appearance of, programme articles by skipper Mackay. Brian ignored the rules in Dave's contract by arranging for him to receive £5 as a backhander for his programme notes. It was entered in the books when Dave got his fiver, but the money should have gone in his wages instead and been subject to income tax. Five pounds. It sounds such a paltry amount now, yet in the summer of 1970 it would have bought a season ticket on the Pop Side terraces at Derby. Petty cash was also shelled out without chits in return, and there was no system for the sale of season tickets.

The harsh penalty was delivered in early April, days after Derby's 2-0 home win over Wolverhampton Wanderers which would, in normal circumstances, have clinched a place in the Fairs Cup, quite an achievement in the club's debut season in the First Division under the Clough-Taylor regime. I learned how everyone at the club was made to sweat over the punishment. Considering the gravity of its contents, you might have thought the relevant letter from Lancaster Gate would have been sent by registered post or recorded delivery. It wasn't, and when frantic enquiries led to a London sorting office, the envelope was dispatched by rail from St Pancras, met at Derby station by Post Office officials and rushed to the Baseball Ground.

Clough rallied his dispirited players to share the honours in the final match of the campaign, 1-1 at Southampton, and secure fourth place in the table. That made it eight wins and four draws in the final 12 matches. No wonder supporters were soon queuing down the street for season tickets.

The manager was obviously trying to establish that he had the total control that he had, in fact, enjoyed now for quite some time. Having made a fortune out of the haulage business, Sam Longson was nobody's fool, but I discovered directors who were local businessmen, basically along for the ride, who didn't understand what the football club was about. Sydney Bradley, for example, was an amiable enough chap who bore a striking resemblance to Arthur Lowe's Captain Mainwaring in *Dad's Army*. He owned one of those traditional "old-fashioned" gents' outfitters in town. Brian, the gunslinger, came in and took over the club and everything else that went with it. But everything changed when the books were opened and the club's dirty laundry received a public airing. Brian didn't take the rap. He got the secretary, 21-year-old Malcolm Bramley, brought in the previous year from Sunderland, Brian's old club, to act as the fall guy. Brian used a contact on *The Sun* for Malcolm to do a piece for them and get paid £200 for the privilege to soften the blow of the sack.

* * * * *

A small, cramped old gymnasium filled with temporary trestle tables acted as the nerve-centre for a huge ticket-selling operation in January 1971 when Derby County were drawn to face Wolverhampton Wanderers in the fourth round of the FA Cup. Earlier that month, Bill McGarry's fine side had beaten us 2-1 before 34,243 spectators at the Baseball Ground. Suddenly, it seemed as if every fan in the Midlands wanted to witness the rematch.

In the event, we squeezed in a crowd of 40,567. In the build-up to the match the premises might have been mistaken for a polling booth at a local school, but there were no ballot boxes, just a collection of green metal wastepaper bins to collect a flood of fivers and one-pound notes, cheques and postal orders. There was no till, no organisation – just chaos. Senior players and apprentice footballers alike were carrying bins full of money from one end of the ground, through a corridor and alongside the pitch to the general office. The contents were counted and bundled up ready for the bank.

SHOOTING STARS

Loyal supporters poured in after queuing outside in Shaftesbury Crescent. Brian, who came in after training, wearing an old tracksuit top, strolled around, shaking hands with those lucky punters who had timed their visit right. He had access everywhere, he was a god, a sort of messiah – and he also took a keen interest in how well the transactions were going.

The people we had selling tickets were kids. There was no proper organisation before I recruited some professional staff from the National Westminster Bank, where the money was eventually heading. Those tellers came in after work at five o'clock to cash up for us. We knew how many tickets we had sold, so the numbers should have tallied, it was easy. However, on this particular day we were out by about 400 quid. So it went on … check, re-check … the team worked through five o'clock, six o'clock, seven o'clock – and they were panicking. Four hundred pounds? Then somebody reminded me: "Oh, that's about what one of those wastepaper bins holds." Welcome to Derby, indeed!

"Who else was in?" I demanded to know.

"Well, the manager was in. I don't know whether he picked one up and took it to the office or not."

There was now general dismay that FA Cup tickets and receipts didn't balance. How could we have missed so much money?

At nine o'clock that evening I packed everybody off home. We were thoroughly fed up.

The following morning, I broadcast the fact that I was going to the police because I suspected that there was a thief in the club. Actually, I went for a haircut instead and returned to the Baseball Ground at about 10.30am. Brian immediately asked me to pop down to his office. "Where have you been, Stuart?" he was eager to know.

"Oh, I've been to the police. We have a problem. We have a thief in the club, there's money missing. It's my responsibility, very worrying."

And, with that, Brian sort of smiled, a half-smile, and opened a desk drawer. I watched as he produced neatly bundled notes, about £400 all told.

He said: "You know, I was just testing you. I was just testing your system."

I replied: "What are you doing that for? It's my job. We're working together. Why would you do that?"

"Oh, I was just testing you to see if your systems were right."

If I hadn't reported the missing money and taken it to the board, Brian could have gone to them complaining about me; if not that then he would always have leverage over me. Or, of course, he could just have taken the money. I didn't know the score for sure, but finding the cash in Brian's drawer shocked me to the core.

I didn't think that anybody in an organisation would want to pull a stunt like that. Indeed, would have the capacity or the audacity to do that. We were all working together. What was the motive? That was what shocked me. Here was someone either trying to trip me up or have some power over me. I became very worried about Brian's persona, what the game was, what he was trying to do. And I was furious. I looked him straight in the eye and said: "If you ever pull anything like that again, I will go straight to the chairman and I won't hesitate to expose you."

SHOOTING STARS

One early board meeting was depressing and gave me an insight into future conflict. Director Bill Rudd, a local solicitor, announced: "We can't sign these accounts because they are incorrect, and because I am unhappy with certain aspects relating to the manager's expenses. Gentlemen, if we do sign these documents, we could all end up in prison." Purely by coincidence, many years later under Brian's stewardship of Nottingham Forest, two of his chairmen did go to jail: Maurice Roworth for fraud; and Stuart Dryden for fiddling the post office where he worked.

2

Press Gang

DRINKING BECAME a way of life for Brian Clough. He would come in before training on a cold morning and be in his office while the players were getting stripped, and he'd say to Peter Taylor: "Let's have a nip," and spice up his mug of coffee with a generous slug of brandy. Brian arguably generated as much, if not more, hype and publicity than all the other First Division managers put together. Consequently, there were always journalists coming in at lunchtime to get a story. Not just the local boys, but also the nationals – the Birmingham brigade, Manchester mob, and Fleet Street up on the train from London.

There was always something happening, and if there wasn't then Brian would think of something to guarantee he made a splash. Training finished for the day, he'd come back to his office for a glass of champagne with the press before a long, leisurely lunch over a couple of bottles of wine at La Gondola, a nearby Italian restaurant. Then the party would carry on back at the ground with another brandy around five o'clock when Brian would give his acolytes what they were after – a story to make all the national newspapers.

Brian was invariably having a pop at somebody and, as a consequence, the club was getting it in the neck from the Football Association or Football League. Or both. Of course, by "the club" I mean individuals. Criticism from the authorities would be levelled at Sam Longson, the chairman, and myself, and all because of the manager's actions over which we had no control.

Brian and Peter Taylor used every situation to try to improve their lot and climb up the ladder. They were successful and, as such, they were being touted around to rival chairmen. Journalists were cooing: "You want to get the lads from Derby, they're the best." It was a mutual arrangement, Brian courting the journalists who, in turn, were happy to promote him. Both he and Peter were more than happy to be put on pedestals.

Brian took advantage of his brilliant success, which most people would do, but he turned it into an art, manipulating the press who were only too pleased to be on his side because he was winning everything in front of him. And all the time he was talking to the press he was winding-up the Football League and the FA. The journalists were hungry for stories, and Brian fed them his opinion on whatever took his fancy. He talked about anything and everything. He loved politics, Harold Wilson, Michael Foot, the Labour Party – he was into all that. Anything that was relevant, he was having a go at. Anything in the game that was relevant, there was always a Brian Clough quote … FA chairman this, Football League secretary that … he was a pain in their backsides.

He would have been a good England manager but the blazers wouldn't have him at any price, because they were terrified of him. The FA called his bluff when he was interviewed at Lancaster Gate for the top job and claimed to be so patriotic he'd do anything for the national cause. So they gave him and Peter the youth team job. Brian got his blazer with the Three Lions badge, said the right thing – that he was honoured – but deep down he thought it was a slap in the face. That association with the England youngsters was short and none too sweet.

Yet the arrogance was occasionally replaced by something more endearing. As Derby closed in on the League title in 1972, I drove with Brian and Peter to Old Trafford to watch a potential signing. About ten minutes before the final whistle, we were leaving the back of the directors' box and climbing down the stairs to the exit when the Manchester United manager turned in his seat at the end of a row to greet us belatedly: "Oh, good to see you, Brian, Peter – thank you for coming." Back in the car, the Derby manager and his assistant were extremely flattered that Matt Busby knew their names. The mood enveloping them was one of "Christ, now we have arrived!" Brian turned to Peter and said: "It's a long way from Hartlepool, eh?"

On one unforgettable occasion in my company, Brian revealed his distaste for rudeness – other people's, at any rate – and his readiness to intervene if he felt that someone was being given a hard time. He and Peter, and their wives Barbara and Lilian, invited Josie and me, along with Mike Keeling, a director, and his girlfriend to a posh, midweek, black-tie dinner at The Savoy in London, where Sacha Distel was providing the cabaret. It was a big night out, a marvellous occasion, excellent food – scampi, steaks, the wine flowing plus a magnum of champagne. It had been Peter's idea; he wanted to bring us all together after the episode with the missing Wolves FA Cup money.

Brian appreciated quality singers. Frank Sinatra, Matt Monro … he loved them and he was very attentive when Sacha started his set. It didn't take long, however, for Brian's mood to darken and just when the French star was launching into one of his biggest hits, *Raindrops Keep Fallin' on My Head*, the noise from the next table, which had been bubbling all evening, suddenly exploded. So did Brian. Up he jumped to wag an admonishing finger at the raucous party and reprimand them loudly: "Hey, give the poor lad a chance, he's working and he's a good singer, you know. Trying to sing for your entertainment." The effect was dramatic. Everything stopped, the band, Sacha Distel, the whole room. Brian became the centre of attention and we didn't hear another peep from that cowed party all night. When we left, I half-expected to see Sacha Distel at the door, asking for Brian's autograph.

He possessed such an aura, people told me they could sense when he walked into a room because the hairs on the backs of their necks stood up. He did a lot of things for charity, he did a lot of things for the miners, all of that, but I can't say there wasn't a motive. He did what he wanted to do – he was that sort.

The players' wives would get bouquets of flowers because he wanted the players to feel happy at home, he wanted the players to perform for him. He cast a spell over them. Sometimes the players were told to meet at the Midland Hotel, say 12 o'clock on Sunday lunchtime, for a get-together, and Brian would suddenly whisk them off to Mallorca for a four-day training break in the sun. He would send the wives bouquets to say: "Sorry, I've taken them away." It was all part of building what he decided was "his club". What a supreme motivator and man-manager he was.

February and March 1972 saw the UK almost brought to its knees by the striking miners, and there was another monumental, protracted power struggle as Derby faced Arsenal over four matches. Bertie Mee's Gunners took the honours in the First Division match, 2-0 at Highbury, with the clubs already knowing that they faced each other again a fortnight later in the fifth round of the FA Cup at the Baseball Ground, a full-blooded 2-2 draw on a mudheap. Because there was no guarantee of electricity to operate floodlights, the replay in London was set for the following Tuesday afternoon. In fact, the miners' strike prompted the Government to ban all floodlit matches.

Such was the dramatic nature of the first game, with Arsenal's two-goal Charlie George at his explosive best amid some X-rated tackles and an 88th-minute penalty equaliser by Alan Hinton, there was huge interest in the outcome and no shortage of supporters with so many people laid off or on shortened working weeks. Our team bus was inching along the side streets of north London, through a crowd which would number 63,077, when Clough spun round from his seat at the front to say: "Hey, Toddy. You come up here." As he sat next to the manager, England international Colin Todd, probably the best defender in the country and arguably the world at the time, was told: "You are the man who will win this game for this team and all these players."

Clough's instinct and rapport with his players enabled him to single out the individual who might be fretting over form or fitness, or the one he sensed could raise his performance and prove decisive. When Alan Hinton went through periods of uncertainty he was told what a great winger he was. Belper-born Ron Webster, a professional at the club since the Harry Storer days of 1960, was reassured that he fully deserved his place at right-back in a team packed with internationals.

On this occasion, even a pumped-up Todd's best wasn't quite enough as two physically shattered and mentally drained sides fought each other to a standstill. Even 30 minutes of extra-time failed to prevent a stalemate. Arsenal went on to win the second replay 1-0 at Leicester City's Filbert Street; Derby County went on to win the title.

Clough pulled his "front of the bus" trick to telling effect the following season when November 1972 found us flying to Portugal to defend what appeared to be a handsome 3-0 first-leg lead over Benfica, Eusebio and all, in the second round of the European Cup. Benfica were unaccustomed to being humiliated in a tournament they had won twice in the 1960s, a decade in which they appeared in no fewer than five finals, and we all knew they would press strongly for an early goal.

If he had any qualms about facing the Portuguese champions in front of a frenzied crowd of 75,000 in the Estadio da Luz, Clough kept them to himself despite taking the precaution of resting Kevin Hector, John O'Hare and Archie Gemmill for the preceding match – a 4-0 defeat at Manchester City. Rather than stay in a lovely, five-star hotel in Lisbon with all the trimmings, Peter Taylor had done a deal with his pal Ernie Clay, a Yorkshire-born businessman who was to become Fulham chairman, to base ourselves in a godforsaken place he owned. It was like a Pontins holiday camp, without the excitement, marooned out in the sticks next to a beach in the middle of nowhere, about an hour-and-a-half's drive from Lisbon.

It turned out beautifully for us, however, and it was just the setting for Peter and Brian to work their magic. Training consisted of the players walking the entire length of the beach, a good three-quarters of a mile, with their tracksuit bottoms rolled up to the knee and their bare feet turning blue in the freezing Atlantic. One or two of the lads were a little apprehensive but when Brian fixed them with a stare and said: "Come on, do join us for a little paddle, it will do you good," they realised it would not be in their best interests to demur. Refreshing stroll over, a treat awaited the team as they were marched into a top-notch seafood restaurant to feast over prawns, lobster and squid for lunch.

Late the following afternoon, Clough prepared for the trip into Lisbon by bringing a crate of beer and several bottles of rosé wine on to the coach, casually telling the players: "If you fancy a drink, help yourselves."

Clough knew Colin Boulton had to be at his sharpest to preserve our three-goal lead, and the goalkeeper was duly summoned to the front. "Sit here, sit with me," said Clough, as everybody else craned their necks – Archie Gemmill, Roy McFarland, Todd, the lot.

"Peter, Colin, have a cigarette," said the manager.

A cigarette? On the team bus? Nobody ever smoked within 100 yards of anybody else. But there's Colin Boulton, sitting there, front of the bus, feet up, with Clough and Taylor, enjoying a cigarette more or less all the way to the stadium. It was the manager's way of telling Boulton – and informing everybody else – that he was the man for the occasion. You could almost hear the other boys' brains working as they wondered: "What's going on here?" And there was Boulton taking full advantage of the situation in front of his mates, smoking ostentatiously, looking back with a huge grin, smiling as if to say: "I'm with the boss here, having a fag. I've made it."

As expected, Benfica pressed furiously with Eusebio in full flow for the first 20 minutes, and Boulton stopped everything. He saved the day, it ended 0-0 and we went through. "What a star," said Clough, rewarding the keeper with a light-hearted swipe across the back of his head. "I told you that you would do it for us."

Brian would defend Alan Hinton to the ends of the earth against criticism that the winger was cowed by over-physical full-backs. "They know nothing, absolutely nothing," he told me of the snipers. "I don't pay Alan Hinton to get stuck in, I pay him for his bravery to go forward at pace and put the ball on our centre-forward's head."

Brian was a dictator alright, but there was often a point to be made, as he did about the importance of discipline and time-keeping when fining a player for opening his mouth. Late for training, the player objected to being fined £10.

Clough: "That's £20 now."

Player: "For what?"

Clough: "Opening your mouth."

Player: "Oh, come on."

Clough: "That's £30."

It got to £40 in front of a stunned, and wisely silent, dressing room. Clough would play off the response of individual players.

He made sure he got that £40 off the player in front of the others – and then slipped it back to him quietly, away from the ground. Alan Hinton tells a similar tale about how he failed to turn up for a cricket match because his car broke down. It proved to be a costly malfunction.

Alan told me: "Cloughie loved his cricket, as you know, and we were laughing and joking in the dressing room the following morning. He came in and swivelled round to stare straight at me with an evil grin on his face before announcing: 'Anyone who doesn't turn up for a cricket match, or a ping-pong match, or a darts match, it's the same as not turning up for a Derby County match and you're fined £10.' I said: 'You have to be joking.' And Clough said: '£20.' It eventually topped out at £25 with Terry Hennessey standing behind Brian, waving his hands at me, and going, 'No, no, no…'"

Peter Taylor could be ferocious in his criticism of the team, and individuals, but he also played the court jester, laughing and joking and bringing everyone down with his sharp, dry humour. It was a double act, and if Brian went too far, then Peter made sure that things did not get completely out of hand. Brian was arrogant in most things he did. Winning the title, he felt he'd reached it then, that he'd made it. He was brazen, and when Coventry City – in the form of chairman Derrick Robins and director Micky French – courted him at the Midland Hotel, Brian took the bill for three bottles of champagne and smoked salmon and charged it to Derby County. Sam Longson went bananas. But Clough still used Coventry's interest to bag a £5,000 pay rise for himself and £3,000 for Taylor.

3
Jumping the Gun

THINK OF Peter Taylor identifying a potential signing, Brian Clough giving his blessing, Derby County requesting permission to discuss terms with the player and the clubs agreeing a transfer fee. Now think again. As orthodox as that scenario might seem, it was anathema to Brian. He lived for the thrill of the chase, gaining an edge, turning someone over, pulling off a coup to leave the biggest clubs in England trailing in his wake while he basked in the limelight ... not to mention paying a fortune. After all, it wasn't his money.

For all their brilliance working the transfer market, the dynamic duo were not infallible and I can modestly claim to have been instrumental in bringing one of Derby County's most successful players to the Baseball Ground. Preston's Archie Gemmill, by his own admission, did little to catch the eye in two games when my club at the time bowed out of the FA Cup, 4-1 on a rock-hard, frosty Derby pitch in January 1970. In fact, the terrier-like Scot limped off 20 minutes from the end of the replay with a damaged thigh. Clough always swore blind he paid £66,000 for Gemmill without first seeing him kick a ball, such was the faith he had in the skill of his partner, Peter Taylor, as a talent-spotter. I assume, though, that Cloughie was at those two Cup matches.

Although he was making a minor splash as a Scotland Under-23 international, by September 1970 Gemmill was in danger of slipping under Derby's radar.

When I joined the club a few months earlier, I told Peter that there was a guy at Deepdale he ought to have a look at. I knew Archie. We'd met when he arrived from St Mirren – he'd started his working life as an apprentice electrician, by the way – to sign for North End.

I knew Peter was the football man when it came to scouting, and was taken aback when he said: "Archie Gemmill? Not interested. Not a priority." His tune changed when I replied: "Well, you soon will be because Everton are more than keen. My wife, Josie, is still living in Preston and rang me to say the word is that Gemmill is going to Goodison Park."

I was well versed in the background linking the Lancashire and Merseyside clubs. Alan Ball senior was the Preston manager; Alan Ball junior, his son and World Cup winner, was a mainstay of the "Holy Trinity" midfield along with Colin Harvey and Howard Kendall at the champions, Everton, where he had the ear of manager Harry Catterick.

"Oh, bloody hell, are they?" said Peter, surprised and excited.

Brian told me: "Do you know what, Stuart? Nothing gets my juices flowing more than knowing I'm in competition with a big club for a player." Taylor, now similarly motivated, needed no persuasion to watch Gemmill in Preston's next match, and liked what he saw, although a few days later, when I enquired: "Archie Gemmill, what's the score?" he told me plainly: "Problem: Brian's looking at other options."

Everything went quiet for a week before something changed Clough's mind. Whether it was the realisation that his partner was very rarely wrong when it came to assessing players, or whether Taylor kept bending his ear, or maybe outside influences endorsed Taylor's verdict, I can't be sure. But there was urgency in Clough's voice when he phoned me one afternoon to say: "Right, we're going up … now."

Peter, Brian and myself drove to the Pack Horse Hotel in Bolton to meet Alan Ball senior and Archie over a bottle of wine, a couple of halves of lager and an orange juice for the teetotal Scot. The Preston manager seemed to enjoy having Clough's undivided attention and smugly told us how a move to Everton was virtually a done deal and just how good a player Archie was. Clough shot him a withering look and said: "Yes, I am aware of that. It's why we have driven here from Derby … to sign him."

Ball thought he could milk the situation, tease and tantalise Clough, and maybe force up the asking price. He was playing a dangerous game, though, and his face crumpled as Archie was informed how successful he would become at Derby. Gemmill was given a nod by Ball to join him in the gents', no doubt to be reminded of the lucrative offer from Everton which would have suited the North End manager, but their conversation was interrupted by Taylor, who eased himself into a stall next to them in the urinals to tell Ball: "You're wasting your time, Alan. The boy will be joining us."

Back at the table, Clough calmly examined his fingernails as Ball blustered about "why not talk to our Alan about all this?" I pulled him up sharply: "What's your Alan got to do with anything? He's at bloody Everton." I excused myself to contact George Haworth, the Preston club secretary, we agreed the fee – £66,000 – and it was left to Gemmill and his pregnant wife, Betty, to decide the next step.

Peter drove home, I stayed with Josie in Preston, and Brian refused to let Archie out of his sight, staying overnight in the Gemmills' guest room down the road at Lytham St Annes on the Fylde coast before joining Archie in a breakfast of bacon and eggs, at which the player signed a batch of transfer forms. An hour later at Deepdale, George Haworth was told by the chairman and Ball to sign nothing because an auction between Derby and Everton might drive up the price.

I got wind of the fact that Harry Catterick was on his way, and knew I had to work fast. I impressed upon George that Preston had accepted Derby's offer. Archie had already signed for us, only wanted to play for us, and after serving North End faithfully he had earned the right to choose his own destiny. With my heart pounding, I whipped out the transfer forms and said: "Just sign here, George, we'll bugger off and you can enjoy the rest of your day." Haworth carefully added his signature, and Brian, Archie and myself walked out of the main door at Deepdale just as the Everton delegation were arriving. Mission accomplished. Phew!

Our manager was very proud of the way he went up to Sunderland on his own in February 1971 and talked his way into buying Colin Todd for £175,000, at that time a British record fee for a defender. Alan Brown had been in charge at

JUMPING THE GUN

Roker Park when Clough was a player there and was back for a second spell. Brian related how he played the innocent, seeking sympathy for Derby's current sticky patch, and agreeing with Brown's prediction that he had a lot to learn if he was to remain in football management. Brown tried to conclude negotiations by claiming all the money in the world could not buy Todd, but Brian persisted that every player had his price. Brown told him it would take £175,000 – and when Brian immediately stuck out his hand and said: "Done!" Cloughie related: "He just couldn't stop a smile, thinking he'd done me as he said '£175,000 for a 22-year-old!' as if I was out of my mind."

When the details of the transfer were revealed, Sam Longson almost choked on his Caribbean lobster dinner in Antigua with Derrick Robins and Arthur Waite, fellow chairmen of Coventry City and Crystal Palace respectively. Until that moment the only intelligence Sam had was a telegram from Cable and Wireless (West Indies) Ltd, addressed "To Longson" and reading: "Signed you another good player. Todd. Running short of cash – BC." He told Sam he'd done it, but he hadn't closed the deal because we hadn't got the money. Sunderland wanted the lot in one payment – and we couldn't fund the transfer. On his return from the Caribbean, Sam told me to go to see our bank manager and sort out an extended overdraft, which, after a few days of negotiations, I did. That was how Cloughie worked. He thought nothing of telling Sam: "Oh, Mr Chairman, I've done this deal. By the way, you've got to pay half-a-million quid by tomorrow."

Peter Taylor was beside himself with anger when he and I paraded Ian Storey-Moore, as he was then known, on the pitch as "Derby County's new player" before a home match against Wolves in March 1972. Four men, two abreast, set out through the corridors of the Baseball Ground to announce the coup to a crowd of 33,456 – but only three arrived in the centre-circle. As we emerged from the tunnel, Brian was nowhere to be seen, and Peter did not hide his anger, hissing at me: "The bastard, he's gone back in the dressing room."

As always, Cloughie had been the prime mover in the deal, but his action, or rather inaction, meant that he had chosen to wash his hands of the showmanship that could get Derby County into hot water with the authorities – because there was one massive stumbling block to the flying winger becoming the final piece in the Rams' title-winning jigsaw: he was still the property of our bitter rivals, Nottingham Forest.

Storey-Moore was a great player, local, good enough to appear for England at a time when caps were not scattered cheaply like confetti. At 28, he was in his prime, although he was unable to prevent Forest sliding towards relegation. He also had first-hand confirmation of where the power now lay in the East Midlands because, a fortnight earlier, Derby had completed the double over the neighbours with a 4-0 win in what proved to be Storey-Moore's final match for Forest. Clough wanted him because he could operate anywhere along the front line – right, left or as a centre-forward. He wanted him because the signing would humiliate Matt Busby and Frank O'Farrell at United. And he wanted Storey-Moore as an "up yours" response to Malcolm Allison, his opposite number at championship rivals Manchester City, who had bought striker Rodney Marsh for £200,000 from QPR to strengthen their hand in the run-in.

JUMPING THE GUN

The City Ground board decided to cash in on their major asset, agreeing to sell Storey-Moore to Manchester United for £200,000. "Over my dead body," shouted Clough when he learned of a talent bound for Old Trafford, and he couldn't drag me quickly enough over to Nottingham's Edwalton Hall Hotel, where the player was hesitating over United's personal terms.

Forest's manager, Matt Gillies, and their secretary, Ken Smales, had no objection to us talking to Storey-Moore. We burst in like a tornado that Friday, Brian working his magic, promising a wide-eyed player the earth in terms of future glory and assuring him of top wages. He was easily persuaded to sign transfer forms, to which I added my signature. Ian Storey-Moore was now effectively a Derby County employee – if Smales signed too. He refused.

I felt sorry for the disconsolate player before Brian wrapped an arm around him and said: "You're coming back to Derby tonight with us to meet the lads and stay in a decent hotel."

The other players warmly welcomed Ian, but in the morning all hell broke loose. The *Daily Mirror*'s back-page headline posed the question: "Who's got Storey-Moore?" and fuelled the mystery by adding: "'Me', says Clough … 'No, I have', says O'Farrell."

Breakfast was barely over when Matt Gillies announced: "As a result of an emergency meeting of the committee, Nottingham Forest have not assented to Ian Storey-Moore's transfer to Derby County. The whole situation regarding his transfer is still under discussion." Clough bristled defiance in his response: "As far as we're concerned, we have signed Storey-Moore, and I am not really concerned what any other party might feel."

I could almost sympathise with the "enemy". Forest were a shambles on the pitch, going down, and their supporters had seen Alan Hinton join us to revitalise his career, and another former player, Frank Wignall, enjoy some great times with us, too. In February 1970 they suffered the embarrassment of losing the highly influential Terry Hennessey to Derby for £100,000, and Clough still fancied Forest old boy Henry Newton, currently at Everton and destined to be his final signing at the Baseball Ground.

Maybe the joke that Forest were becoming a feeder club for Derby finally struck a nerve in their committee room that weekend. I think there was confusion at Forest, some committeemen feeling that Storey-Moore's loyalty — he had scored over 100 goals in more than 230 games – to the Garibaldi red for ten years entitled him to choose his next employers, while others feared that if he joined us then there would be a backlash, rebellion on the terraces, not to mention some sort of legal action from Manchester United. Certainly, it would sit better with everyone at the City Ground if the cheque they received came from Manchester rather than from Derby.

When a television reporter buttonholed Clough with Storey-Moore as they went into the Midland Hotel for a bite to eat, he said: "He's a Derby player and was a Derby player at approximately seven o'clock last night." Asked why there was a suggestion that he had given an undertaking to join Manchester United, the player replied: "I don't know anything about that. All I know is that I've joined a great club." A couple of hours later, a tetchy, terse Clough, almost in the mood for a fight, emerged from the Midland to head for the match, only to discover TV cameras staking out the hotel.

JUMPING THE GUN

Risking Brian's verbal wrath, or worse, a brave reporter approached him and announced: "The Forest committee have held a meeting and they say the deal is off." Clough, his patience painfully thin as he pushed his way to his Mercedes, replied: "Not again, please. I'm not interested in what Notts Forest's committee has to say at all. I am not interested in what anybody has to say. I told you before lunch and I'm telling you again – he signed for Derby County at seven o'clock last night. Please do not waste my time again by asking me the same questions."

The saga threatened to overshadow the match against Wolves, and Peter Taylor asked Brian and myself: "How are we going to sort this out?"

"Well, it's going to be difficult," I said. "We'll have to wait and do it Monday morning." Peter wasn't keen, fearing the FA would get involved and, given Derby's track record with the authorities, the result would be unfavourable. Then he had what we thought was a brainwave: "What about walking him on to the pitch, telling the fans he's ours in front of the press and TV cameras?"

That was Peter's suggestion. Brian was there. He smiled broadly and gave a one-word response: "Great."

I collared the bloke who announced the teams, and revealed our plan. Storey-Moore came out of the dressing room, where he had been watching his proposed new teammates get changed, to join Clough, Taylor and myself.

Both teams ran out, the four of us started to follow them, and the atmosphere turned electric as a voice boomed over the music: "Please put your hands together for our new signing, England international, Ian Storey-Moore, who will be joining the club." And out we walked into the arena. Well, three of us did.

Cloughie's not there. I looked round – he's gone. He didn't walk. The bastard was back in the dressing room. So we're walking to the centre-circle, Peter, Ian and me, waving to the crowd, and Peter's looking at me and asking out of the side of his mouth: "Where is he?" Then it dawned on Peter that if anyone was going to be held accountable for Derby County flouting regulations, Clough didn't intend it to be him. Peter said to me: "The bastard. He's done it again. Done us like a kipper!"

A photograph speaks volumes for how the three of us felt. There is a happy Ian Storey-Moore, his hands raised in response to adulation from the terraces, with Peter and myself wearing sheepskin coats and the pained expressions of men who have just discovered they have been hung out to dry. We walked back, Peter to confront Brian and, in his words, "Find out just what the fuck he thinks he's playing at"; me to my office; and Ian to Gordon Guthrie, our physio, who would find him a seat in the directors' box. "You'll be all right with Gordon," I said, but I feared Peter and I would suffer reprisals because every newspaper used the photograph of the pair of us waving to the crowd with "our new signing" Ian Storey-Moore – who was still a Nottingham Forest player. The shit duly hit the fan, Ken Smales phoning after Derby's 2-1 win to inform me: "You have broken every rule in the book. He's our player, I've reported you to the FA."

Clough made sure Storey-Moore, now joined by his wife, spent Saturday night in Derby at the Midland Hotel in an effort to somehow force the issue and make it difficult for United to reach him. But our influence began to wane, Ian started to twitch, nervous, lonely, isolated, no longer surrounded by football people, the Derby team and 33,000 supporters. He called me and said: "This has gone on long enough, Stuart. What's happening?" I couldn't give him a straight answer. It was as if grains of sand were slipping through my fingers. Late on Sunday afternoon I got another call: The couple were going home to Bingham, with a view to Ian talking to another club on Monday morning. We made another desperate attempt to get Forest's blessing, but they were adamant: He wasn't going to Derby. Matt Busby arrived in Bingham with a handsome bouquet of flowers for Mrs Storey-Moore, and that was it, job done. Ian Storey-Moore was a Manchester United player.

The *Daily Mirror* told readers: "Storey-Moore changes mind ... on his wife's orders. Why Ian signed for United by Mrs Storey-Moore." On television she revealed: "Ian is the boss. I've always gone by Ian's decisions, but I felt it was time I intervened to a certain extent. I don't interfere with his football in any way but where our personal happiness is concerned I felt it was my duty as a wife to have him here and give him a chance to think clearly and decide what he wanted to do."

The wrath of the FA came down on me in the shape of a four-page letter condemning Derby County for, as Ken Smales complained, "breaking every rule in the book". An official enquiry followed and the club was fined £5,000.

Peter felt Brian was guilty of dereliction of duty, but after his brief outpouring of bile there was no lasting resentment, just acceptance. "He's done it again," said Taylor, shrugging his shoulders. It was one of maybe a dozen occasions when Brian "played" his partner and chose to put him in an embarrassing position as we looked to negotiate a deal. "You go, you go and represent the club if you're so bloody keen," Clough would say, cruelly on occasions, knowing full well that Taylor shunned the limelight on his own.

Perhaps their most spectacular fall-out came in April 1973, when Derby were in Turin to face the biggest game in the club's history – Juventus in the semi-final first leg of the European Cup. Two nights before the match, to entertain the travelling English press corps, I had arranged a themed dinner with the management and directors, with traditional Italian dishes and superb wines on the menu.

It must have been about four in the afternoon after training and all the players were relaxing in the hotel lounge, playing cards with Brian, when Peter asked me: "What time are we going? What time do you want us there?"

"Relax, Peter," I told him. "We're leaving at 6.30, so there's plenty of time."

He was keen to know the dress code, and I said it would be collar and tie, Derby County blazer, because it was a club function and I felt that it was important, as England's champions, to dress the part on a foreign mission, and fly the flag.

The players were given the evening off to carry on with their card school and have a bite to eat – and a beer or two in moderation – in the hotel. At 6.15pm everyone but Brian was down in the lobby, directors and senior staff ready for taxis, blazers on, boots blacked, looking the part. At 6.30pm there was still no Brian. The taxis were ready, engines running. I said to Peter: "Where's Brian?" But before he could reply, one of the players reassured us: "The gaffer's only just packed in cards; he's gone up to get changed." Fair enough, I thought. Then Brian appeared, bounding down the stairs, rubbing his hands, smiling broadly, and still wearing his sweaty tracksuit from training.

It was petty stuff, but Cloughie was a law unto himself. I thought if he wanted to be different, what did it matter? None of the press lads would raise an eyebrow or criticise him. They were all his mates. But Peter went ballistic and the pair of them started arguing. The dispute escalated into a full-blown row of unimaginable proportions, a serious row, and it carried on for a long time. It became a shouting match, horrendous, not at all healthy. That was the biggest row I ever witnessed between them.

What was Brian playing at? Peter thought that he was trying to assert his authority, his superiority. On the face of it the manager had cut it fine playing cards with the players, gone up to his room, and thought: "Oh, sod it. I'm not going to get changed. It's only a dinner with press, they are all my mates anyway."

Peter had bothered to make an effort, however: he'd showered and put on his best bib and tucker like the rest of us. Now he was left feeling foolish, undermined in a hotel lobby. They were supposed to be partners, but Brian's tracksuit at the dinner would give the impression that here was the hard-working manager in charge of the team, while Peter was done-up and might have passed as an anonymous club director. Brian could very easily have told Peter: "Webby wants us to dress up for the board, but I can't be bothered. Let's just wear our tracksuits and we'll be off."

But he didn't. He was always different and always wanted to be different. Later at the dinner, Peter looked me straight in the face and said: "Some bloody partner I've got, eh? He's a law unto himself, that one. Even I can't work him out half the time, and I'm his best pal."

4
Title and Tantrums

OF COURSE it wasn't all bitterness and bile, and when Brian Clough and Peter Taylor were in perfect harmony it was like football's equivalent to watching André Previn conducting the London Symphony Orchestra – the very sweetest music. Or sometimes it more resembled Morecambe and Wise on stage. Either way, there was rarely a dull moment. And there was almost always something to cheer.

That fabulous European Cup adventure, which ended on such a sour note against Juventus, was still a pipedream for much of Derby County's historic 1971-72 season. When the team went unbeaten in the opening dozen matches of the First Division campaign, I sensed that we could be in for something a bit special, certainly qualification for the UEFA Cup and the financial rewards that would bring the club.

But as autumn turned to winter, our away form fell away like leaves off the trees in Markeaton Park. It looked like being a very costly period. The game at relegation-haunted Huddersfield Town on 27 November was a horrific afternoon, and when Cloughie and Pete, faces like thunder, descended into the away dressing room at Leeds Road, I knew that the mother and father of all bollockings was arriving with them.

On the coach trip home after a 2-1 defeat the atmosphere was so quiet and sombre, you'd have been forgiven for thinking we were a party of Trappist monks. I asked one of the players what had happened, and he told me: "I think Huddersfield will be having the decorators in on Monday. The gaffer stripped the paint off the walls with his tongue. He said if we don't all get stuck in, we can all fuck off."

The message took some time to sink in, and exactly one month later, 27 December, brought more disappointment as we went down 3-0 at Elland Road to a Leeds United side managed by Don Revie, a man for whom Brian had the utmost contempt – although he did confide in me: "We could do with a few with their balls; they're quite handy when they're not kicking lumps out of you."

Either Brian or Don was going to end up with egg on his face on All Fools' Day at the Baseball Ground, and it was Revie as John O'Hare took a starring role in our excellent 2-0 victory, making Jack Charlton and Norman Hunter (who was pressured into scoring an own-goal) look ordinary. We were top of the table.

I felt the exhilaration that day, but shared in the abject despair two days later when mid-table Newcastle United did the virtually unmanageable and won at the Baseball Ground – the only club to achieve that feat all season. Brian rewarded the players with a tirade of Huddersfield proportions.

Lesser characters might have wilted under the pressure, not to mention the personal abuse, but this Derby side was full of men, real men who knew exactly what the manager was about and, if stick was dished out, they bloody well knew they had to take it or start looking for another job.

A goalless draw at West Bromwich Albion was barely acceptable but hope was restored thanks to two handsome wins – 4-0 at Sheffield United and 3-0 at home to bottom-of-the-table Huddersfield.

The very last lap of the championship run-in approached and I was so tense that I was off my food to the extent that Josie feared I was developing an ulcer. In truth, more than a few people at the club were drinking a bit too much to calm their nerves and to try to convince themselves that there were some things in life more important than football. As if! It was now a four-horse race between ourselves, Leeds, Liverpool and Manchester City. A sunny 22 April saw our supporters packed on to the club's Ramaway train to Manchester Piccadilly, while a convoy of coaches and cars also headed north-west for the date with Malcolm Allison's City.

The Derby rollercoaster lurched horribly downwards again as City – inspired by their £200,000 signing Rodney Marsh, reintroduced to the side after turning up from QPR plainly unfit – stuffed us 2-0. The atmosphere in the Maine Road boardroom was strange and strained after what was City's final match of the season. Yes, they were top with 57 points, but Big Mal knew they could not become champions because of their inferior goal-average. Rival directors smiled at each other and shrugged their shoulders, as if to say: "Close, but no cigar" … apart from

TITLE AND TANTRUMS

a large Havana to go with trademark fedora hat for Malcolm Allison, of course.

Bill Shankly's Liverpool had 56 points from 40 matches, while we had 56 from 41, and Leeds, the bookies' favourites, 55 from 40. Sir Alex Ferguson would later coin the phrase "squeaky bum time", but squeaky wasn't the half of it.

On Monday, 1 May, Liverpool arrived at the Baseball Ground for our final game of the season. I felt a creeping sense of unease before lunch when news filtered through that Ronnie Webster, our ultra-reliable right-back, was unfit. That was not what you wanted to hear when the opposition boasted forwards of the calibre of Kevin Keegan, John Toshack and Steve Heighway. Clough responded to the crisis by turning to 16-year-old Steve Powell, who had experienced a very brief taste of first-team football months earlier, and the raw teenager met the call to arms by playing with the discipline, skill and talent of a seasoned professional. Magnificent.

John McGovern might have gone on to lift a couple of European Cups for Nottingham Forest, but he will always be revered among Derby fans of a certain vintage as the man whose goal effectively won us the title. It was tight, it was tense, I felt the claustrophobia of an intense Baseball Ground crowd of more than 39,000, most of them shoehorned on to those cramped terraces on a warm spring evening, was almost overpowering. McGovern was not noted for his scoring ability. Brian told me: "He'll get me one or two a year, and I'm happy with that. What young McGovern has mastered is the art of stopping the other lot playing. If you come off the pitch wondering if Alan Ball was ever on it to start with, well that's because young McGovern has done his job. And that's why I pay him, Stuart." I did point out to Clough that it was actually Derby County who paid McGovern his wages, but he wasn't listening. By then I was talking to the back of his head as he strode off down the corridor.

So it wasn't Kevin Hector, John O'Hare, Alan Hinton or even Roy McFarland who popped up on the fringe of the Liverpool penalty area in the 62nd minute, when Alan Durban dummied a pass from Archie Gemmill, but McGovern, who fizzed a rising shot past the England goalkeeper, Ray Clemence, before ending up on his backside.

Cloughie whisked his clan off to the Scilly Isle of Tresco for a well-deserved holiday, while Peter and I flew to Cala Millor on Mallorca with the players to await our fate in seven days' time. They say a week is a long time in football, now it felt to me like an eternity until 8 May. Yes, we were top, but Liverpool and Leeds were still fancied to finish first. We were almost out with the washing with the bookies at 8-1. We had run our race, we were in the clubhouse, top of the leaderboard, having birdied the last – but it felt like Jack Nicklaus and Lee Trevino were storming up the 18th fairway.

They were a good bunch, all big characters in their own way. Colin Todd had a quiet authority; Alan Durban and Alan Hinton chatted away to the fans; Roy Mac was a born leader. The punters staying in our hotel were impressed, and they weren't just Derby fans but football supporters in general.

He might have been 850 miles away, but the players were still conscious of Clough's grip because he'd warned them: "You may be on your holidays but, remember, you are still Derby County players and I expect you to behave appropriately." The lads were

TITLE AND TANTRUMS

scattered among the holidaymakers in small groups, enjoying a well-earned San Miguel or three, when word reached us of the results back home in England. Pete and I were having dinner on our own together in the hotel, and we knew something special had happened when the head waiter wandered over, beaming, with a very expensive bottle of Rioja. Leeds had been beaten 2-1 at Wolves, and Liverpool held to a 0-0 draw by Arsenal.

Derby County were champions of England.

Writing those words, saying them aloud, still gives me goosebumps. Little old Derby had defied what bit of logic there is in football, they had beaten all the odds. It felt like Mallorca was suddenly the centre of the world. The hotel telephones were going crazy as family and well-wishers rang to make sure the news had been conveyed. There were no mobile phones, just everyone queuing in reception to call home. Beer flowed, as did the sangria and bubbly. It was an incredible night set against a wonderful buzz of a great party. Champagne corks popped, drinks were downed – a truly fantastic shindig. We hadn't dared organise anything formal, it was all off the cuff and that's what made it even more special. We partied through the night. I'm certain a lot of the Derby fans on the island carried on through the next 24 hours as well.

Cloughie was collared in Tresco and, barely resisting one of his trademark smirks, he told the world: "It is incredible. I do not believe in miracles, but one has occurred tonight. I believe they played four-and-a-half minutes of injury time at Molineux – it seemed like four-and-a-half years to me. There is nothing I can say to sum up my feelings adequately, although I suppose we could have won the FA Cup as well. For a team and a town like Derby to win the title is a credit to all concerned. This has given me far more pleasure than I can adequately express. It makes you appreciate what a job you and your players have done. And my players have given blood this season. In fact, no team has given more."

The following morning gave us chance to regroup somewhat and, one by one, various media parties arrived. ITV sent a crew out straight away, swiftly followed by journalists from each of the national newspapers, but any hopes the media boys had of it being one big jolly for them were cut short when we decided to bring forward our return flight. I spoke on the telephone with Sam Longson, and the chairman agreed that we should do something special at the Baseball Ground with the fans. It seemed only right to celebrate with them, so we flew back into East Midlands Airport and went straight to the stadium where Sam, his fellow board members, Brian, and all the wives were waiting to greet us with thousands of jubilant supporters. It was a wonderful period and, looking back, it's hard to imagine that things would turn so sour between Brian, Peter and the board.

But turn sour they most certainly did – and in next to no time at all.

* * * * *

Success on the field was mirrored by our commercial success. As the players counted their win bonuses, I was as proud of everything I was achieving in helping the club grow. I was confident that I had a lot to offer the football club – in fact the sport – in that respect, and many of the initiatives and ideas that I introduced at Derby County are in place at clubs up and down the land today.

TITLE AND TANTRUMS

In May 1971, a year before we were crowned champions, I oversaw the launch of *The Ram*, the club newspaper. Today clubs have digital departments and TV channels, and the reach of the Internet, but back then, of course, there was no such technology. I just wanted to reach out to fans, to create a family, so I brought in Harry Brown, who had been the editor of the *Football League Review*, and got him to come to work at Derby. Harry was a loveable old rascal, not averse to a drop of scotch and a cigarette, but he was a good professional and a great innovator. Matchday programmes had been around for decades, but I wanted something different, better, and *The Ram* did exceptionally well.

However, I had to fight a lot of people to get that launched, and Clough wasn't happy at the idea of writing a regular column for it. He wanted to save all of his headline-catching opinions for the national press, for TV, knowing full well how that supplemented his salary, but eventually we convinced him to play ball. To be fair, Sam Longson liked *The Ram* and backed me but, like Cloughie, the rest of the directors were a nightmare. They were entrenched in their conservative ways, they didn't embrace change, and this was a new idea. But I fought them all the way, the paper came out and it did well. Our supporters loved the idea of being able to buy it from the newsagent on a Friday morning along with their *Daily Mirror* to read at home.

The introduction of the club shop, the Ramtique, at the Baseball Ground was another excellent revenue stream and then, of course, we set up the Junior Rams. I knew it was crucial to entice our next generation of supporters and a kids' club seemed the perfect way of doing that. These days, a club such as Manchester United will have a small army of at least 30 members of staff working in such departments – that's how seriously they take it. We were trailblazers, the first to set up a scheme that would make Derbyshire's youngsters feel part of the club. As ever, where we led others followed, and six months later Manchester City set up a kids' club of their own. But we had stolen a march on our rivals and soon had 5,000 Junior Rams on board, all of whom received cards on their birthdays and at Christmas. Like hell I was going to lose those fans to Forest, United, Liverpool or Leeds, and I thought the Junior Rams was the perfect way to ensure that didn't happen. Boys and girls were made to feel part of the club's fabric at an early age and became supporters for life. When I see the 25,000, 30,000-plus crowds recorded at the iPro Stadium these days, I'm certain the Junior Rams initiative played its part.

Not long after we started the club, John Motson, the legendary BBC commentator, brought his young son, Fred, to a game. Motty wanted Fred to support Arsenal, but we gave him a Rams presentation pack, had him complete a form, and got him early. Whenever I see him, Motty still kills me for it: "Christ, you *made* him become a Rams supporter!" I did as well.

The Ramaway, the train that took supporters to away matches, was another successful initiative we launched, and we followed that up with the introduction of the Roadrider fans' bus. Derby County were winning matches and we needed – and thanked – the manager and the players for that, but we also needed to create an identity off the field as well. What was the point in allowing fans to spend their money on Trent Buses to take them to away matches when we could do it ourselves? They could all travel together on a club-arranged coach, and for good measure we'd give them all a cuddly Ram toy each when they got on board.

TITLE AND TANTRUMS

Were we exploiting fans? Well, it worked for us, but we were making them feel an important part of the club. It was their club – family, win, lose or draw. I've always felt that when you're part of something like that, then the good times are good and the bad times aren't so bad because you're all in it together, and I didn't want to lose that comradeship and sense of belonging.

What we were doing was innovative in the United Kingdom. I'd go to the United States on holiday and look round their sports stadiums to see what kind of things they were doing. Josie and I visited places such as New Orleans and other major cities, and I had my eyes opened to the opportunities out there. I saw there was more to the game than what we had.

I must confess that I would be lying if I said I saw what the game would become, even years later. When I sat upon the interview panel to appoint the chief executive of the Premier League, then the Premiership, in 1992 there was no telling the monster into which it would grow, but I did see that there was a huge potential for growth.

The success I enjoyed with Derby County wasn't lost on others. When he was a director at Stamford Bridge, the late, great actor and film director Dickie Attenborough came to see me to ask if I would consider going to work for Chelsea. Brian Mears, the Chelsea chairman, flew Josie and I back from a holiday in Barbados to London for talks. I also met the Everton owner, John Moores, in Liverpool during that period. Disney approached me as well. We were doing things that nobody else was doing, punching so far above our weight financially, and, given the capacity at the Baseball Ground, everyone else sat up and took notice. Disney, in particular, saw we were growing commercially and creating a family, and they were impressed with what I was doing. But I wouldn't have understood their work or business model.

Matt Busby would collar me when I visited Josie's parents at their home in Kings Road, Chorlton-cum-Hardy, Manchester – just across the road from where he lived – and politely ask how we, as a small-town club, managed to generate such impressive revenues and punch mightily above our weight. The Manchester United icon was such a wonderful man and I really enjoyed our chats, even if they did leave him scratching his head and still wondering how Derby County prospered.

I loved what I was doing, I understood football and its potential commerce – and I still do.

* * * * *

The incredible scenes that played out in Italy in the spring of 1973, when Derby County were on the wrong end of a blatant piece of bribery, could have been straight from the script of a Hollywood thriller. At half-time the Juventus substitute, Helmut Haller, enjoyed a good laugh and a joke with the referee, Gerhard Schulenburg, his fellow German … a bloody good joke, as it turned out, at our expense.

John Charles, the Wales colossus, travelled with us to Turin for our European Cup semi-final first leg. Charles had spent five successful years with Juventus – they called him "Il Gigante Buono" (The Gentle Giant) – and the hero-worshipping Juve fans treated him like returning royalty. It was King John who tipped off Peter Taylor and me at half-time in the Stadio Comunale that he had spotted Haller entering the referee's room, which was, of course, strictly out of bounds to any player.

TITLE AND TANTRUMS

During the first half we had already seen the two players who'd been carrying yellow cards from our quarter-final victory over Spartak Trnava – Roy McFarland and Archie Gemmill – booked for very little at all. Neither Roy nor Archie was the sort to walk on eggshells, but neither were they the type to go gung-ho in the circumstances, painfully aware as they were that the consequence of another booking would mean they missed the European Cup semi-final second leg at the Baseball Ground. But within the first 45 minutes both had been cautioned. Archie was booked for a retaliatory trip on Giuseppe Furino after the Italian's elbow had smashed into his face, while Roy Mac was cautioned for an accidental clash of heads.

Of course it smelled fishy, and when John told Peter and me about Haller's visit to Schulenburg during the break, our worst fears appeared to be confirmed. We informed the FIFA delegate, and the UEFA delegate, but it appeared that nobody wanted to listen. Unsurprisingly, Peter was furious: "That bastard Haller is in the dressing room with the referee. What the fuck is he doing in there? We got to be careful, here. Very, very careful."

There were one or two murmurings that we might not go out for the second half, in protest that the referee had been nobbled, but eventually we decided the team would go out and finish the game and we would later make our complaints through official channels.

What happened that night was a disgrace ... and worse was to follow. We discovered through the journalist Brian Glanville that the notorious Hungarian fixer, Dezso Solti, the mysterious man in the middle who was representing Juventus, had got hold of the Portuguese referee, Francisco Lobo, ahead of the second leg and told him there was a Fiat car all ready for him to drive home after the match if Juve's safe passage to the final was assured.

The referee went to FIFA and told them of the approach, but FIFA gave him the game at Derby anyway, knowing very well that, although Juventus had tried to bribe him, it couldn't be proved. He would, though, be under the spotlight.

There was always the middleman who wasn't connected with the club, but of course always is: he's the guy off the street, the Italian waiter, whoever. There's next to no way of proving a link, even though everyone knows that there is one. The fact that Señor Lobo informed FIFA of the approach demonstrated that he was thoroughly honest and fair, and he did award us a penalty in the second leg although Alan Hinton missed it as we slipped out of the competition.

Who knows what would have happened had Roy and Archie not been booked in that first leg and been allowed to play in the return; what would have happened had it been a level playing field?

Glanville picked up the story and tried to run with it for a while but he couldn't quite get behind it enough to have Juve thrown out of the tournament. Things were happening above our heads, spinning round, and there was nothing we could do about it. From the moment that Big John told us that he'd seen their lad going into the referee's room we'd known something was wrong. I sat in the stand, gazing down, watching the whole farce play out, and there was nothing that I, or anyone else linked to Derby County, could do about it.

You heard about things like this happening in football. There were always suspicions that it was going on in Italy. But you

TITLE AND TANTRUMS

never expected it to hit you in the face. Yet it did back in 1973 – smack, bang on the end of the nose and, even though we appealed about the skullduggery, we got nowhere. The referee knew he had to book those two players, they were one yellow short of a suspension, and he did, taking them out of the second leg.

Famously, in Turin, Brian stuck his head out of our dressing room and left the throng of Italian journalists who had gathered to talk to him in no doubt whatsoever how he felt about the situation.

"No cheating bastards do I talk to, I will not talk to any cheating bastards," he barked, and with that he closed the door behind him. A second or two later, he re-emerged and addressed the multi-lingual Glanville, who had also been waiting for a word from our manager. "Tell them what I said, Brian!" Then, slam, he disappeared again. Later, when Clough was in a reflective mood, he said to me: "You know what, Stuart? We were babes in the wood." It was an unbelievable episode. Derby County were as close to becoming European champions as we'd ever been or ever have been since.

* * * * *

Not every journey embarked upon by Brian and Peter ended in quite so much acrimony. They often whisked the players away for a few days on a whim and those trips would be immeasurable in terms of creating and harnessing team spirit. I say a whim. It might have seemed like that to everyone else at the club, but the two of them almost always had an ulterior, pre-determined motive for arranging one of their jolly boys' outings, Pete in particular.

"Win today and we're all going to Blackpool!" How many times did I hear him promise? That or a jaunt to Skegness. Peter would dangle the carrot, the lads would go out and do the business, and I'd be there, ducking and diving through the exhaust fumes outside the Baseball Ground as the coach pulled away, trying to appease a collection of bemused wives. Brian would often go bolder: "Two points today and we're off to Mallorca." Funnily enough, I don't remember us losing even one game that had been preceded by that promise.

Nowadays players can afford to charter private jets to whisk them away straight after a game. On a Saturday night they'll go partying in Paris, Barcelona, Ibiza, just hours after competing in a Premier League fixture, and be back again in time for training on a Monday. But in the early 1970s the whole team would go off together and there would be no room for negotiation about staying behind. Not that any of the lads ever really wanted to.

"Scarborough?" I'd ask, as Peter asked me to sign off the expenses for another getaway. "What are you going to Scarborough for?"

"Fresh air, a walk along the seafront and a bag of fish 'n' chips," he'd tell me, and he wouldn't be lying, either. They would go for that little wander along the promenade, lunch wrapped in yesterday's newspaper with a Clough headline dominating the back page. But what Pete had failed to mention ahead of that trip in particular was the fact he'd just bought an apartment in Scarborough and the bus we'd hired would also be used to take up some of his furniture. "Rams Removals" the lads called those trips, and they lapped up the novelty and camaraderie. Episodes like that are all part of the fun and games that go on inside football clubs and, when you're winning, no one gives a monkey's. Not really. Little stunts like that bring everyone together and the more they happened the more everyone loved the manager and his assistant for it.

Pete's brother, Don, and a club scout, Maurice Edwards, sometimes travelled as part of the group. It was a jolly boys' outing with Don and Maurice very close to Peter, who lapped up their chat and company. Senior staff and family were also more than welcome on bonding days out. It all added to the Derby scene at that time, fostering family values, loyalty and success. While Peter kept in touch with his family, so did Brian. For many years, his brother, Barrie, worked as maintenance manager at the Baseball Ground.

Wherever Brian and Peter went they made new disciples, followers who would worship the ground they walked on, and a lot of the time they didn't even have to leave Derby to get their hands on the freshest fish, the best cheeses, the finest malts and wines. Good folk would always be dropping presents off for them at the Baseball Ground, and on a Monday morning after a game in particular the corridors could resemble Billingsgate and Smithfield markets as locals left gifts picked up from all corners of the UK on weekend travels.

"You're going up to Grimsby, you say? Bring us back some fish. Fleetwood? Same again. Somerset? We'll have some cheese. Scotland? A wee dram or two." They'd put their orders in and people couldn't wait to tell the local fishmonger in whichever town they'd headed to that they were buying a little something for Brian Clough and Peter Taylor. Of course, dropping that name guaranteed that the fishmonger would always find the freshest catch. "Ooh, that cod was the best I've tasted," Peter would coo, and a few weeks later there'd be even more boxes of the stuff piled high and stinking the place out. To get to our offices we'd be clambering over sacks of potatoes and vegetables. It was gifts for "The Gods" who were revered by their adoring fans. They were heady days indeed.

But I never once heard Sam complain. It was all part of life in that era, getting away with a team bus to Scarborough to move your furniture, getting something, anything, for nothing, situations that created a bellyful of laughter – and all of it harnessed team spirit wonderfully well.

5

You Can't Win 'Em All, Brian

WHEN THE final whistle sounded at Old Trafford on Saturday, 13 October 1973, Brian Clough felt invincible. He loved nothing more than beating Manchester United, and Kevin Hector's goal in the fourth minute did the trick in United's own backyard.

It was Derby County's first away win of the season, we were up to third in the table, yet the bickering and backstabbing behind the scenes represented a family at war. The afternoon itself had been tainted by a squabble over our allocation of tickets for the directors' box, followed by a dismissive V-sign flicked in that direction by Brian on his way back to the dressing room – although it was never established whether the insult was intended for Sir Matt Busby or our chairman, Sam Longson, who were seated close together.

And there was soon tension in the air when Clough and Peter Taylor appeared in the United boardroom for a post-match beer, the pair standing apart from the Derby directors and myself and glowering in our direction while Sir Matt was busy playing the role of peacemaker Henry Kissinger. If looks could kill, the manager and his assistant would have been on a multiple murder charge. Nothing, however, could prepare me for the storm that broke over the Baseball Ground the following Monday, when politics, a power struggle and pressure came to a head. Poison was dripping off the walls.

* * * * *

Rows had been escalating for weeks, if not months, with Clough spending days out of Derby's loop being outspoken to the delight of London Weekend Television's bigwigs for their *On The Ball* and *Big Match* programmes, and to the dread of Sam and the board, who began to fear repercussions for the club every time the manager opened his mouth. In the *Sunday Express,* for instance, Clough savaged Don Revie's Leeds United over their methods and professionalism, he mocked the 'befuddled' Football Association for failing to impose a telling deterrent, and he called for the Elland Road club to be relegated and their manager heavily fined "to cure many of the ills of the game at a stroke". He was charged with bringing the game into disrepute. "It's all getting too much, Stuart," Sam told me, wearily. "The authorities are sharpening their knives. If we don't rein Brian in, then they are going to come after us. We could face another lengthy ban."

Clough's anger was stoked when the directors locked their drinks cabinet. They were concerned about the amount of booze that Brian and Peter were getting through. Brian was drinking heavily. He'd have a couple of Scotches first thing in the morning and entertain his friends until late at night. His office doubled as the boardroom, where there was a bar with a constant supply of bottles, topped up weekly by club staff. He wanted me sacked for physically applying the lock, but Longson told him I had merely been carrying out instructions. Brian gave me a bitter verbal bashing. I held my hands up in mock surrender and told him: "Don't shoot the messenger."

As a rapid afterthought, and in an attempt to defuse a very tense situation, not to mention a very angry Clough, I added: "Let's have a drink!" but he didn't see the funny side of it and responded with a stare as if I was offering him a large glass of arsenic.

The stakes increased when the managerial duo flew to Amsterdam to watch Holland entertain Poland in a friendly so that Clough, now wearing his hat as a television pundit, could do his homework on behalf of ITV for the forthcoming England-Poland World Cup qualifier at Wembley. Clough had his passport stamped while under no illusions that either he or ITV should be paying for the jaunt, and that the time away would constitute part of his annual leave. But he still submitted a bill for the trip to the club, and Longson almost chewed through a cigar as he tore the paperwork in two and binned it.

I found it tragic to watch the chairman and manager plumb the depths of incompatibility. Neither of them could do anything without arousing something approaching paranoia in the other, trying to second-guess motives. It was almost surreal. Back in the real world, I was shopping in Derby with Josie when an elderly supporter, wearing a black and white scarf, grabbed me by the arm and said: "Congratulations. Delighted to see the club doing well, Mr Webb. It's great for the town." I would have broken his heart if I'd told him the truth. All that loyal fan could see was that Liverpool, the League champions, had been taken apart 3-1, Southampton slaughtered 6-2, and Henry Newton, an immensely capable defensive midfield player, purchased for £100,000 from Everton as Clough sensed the need to return to the clean sheets and consistency which had formed the bedrock of Derby's title-winning season in 1971-72.

But back at the Baseball Ground it was all about power: who was the stronger man, Longson or Clough? Brian believed it was him because he had the publicity, he had the press, he had the dressing room, he had the fans, he was the people's champion, he was the man, he thought he was Robin Hood – and he dismissed the board as insignificant local businessmen trying to stop him. "They don't know the difference between a player and an armchair," he scoffed.

And yet here he was, being cautioned: "Don't do this or that, don't go on TV, don't criticise the FA, don't criticise Alan Hardaker [the Football League secretary]." Brian wanted to talk about the issues of the day. His powers of oratory equipped him to be a first-class politician. He felt he had a question and answer to put to everything ... and he argued that no one had the right to stop him. "Last time I looked it was a free country," he informed me. Free for him, maybe, but there was always a bill to pay. Brian Clough never picked up the tab. It was always the club.

It was interesting, of course. People wanted to hear his views. But you couldn't be a club manager and act in such a provocative, controversial manner. He forgot he had a responsibility to his employers, Derby County, and the FA constantly pilloried the club following his actions. Poor Sam. Every time he went away, other chairmen lectured him. "How can you put up with that manager of yours, the idiot? We wouldn't put up with him, we wouldn't have him in our club." They were either being mischievous or lying, because a great many clubs craved the stardust that Brian Clough was capable of sprinkling. Who knows? If they did their little bit to destabilise us, maybe Brian would join them. So that became external pressure building up on Sam, and he didn't know what to do. Brian was demanding extra money and perks, demanding this, that and the other.

So confident was Brian in his own powers of persuasion that he must have been surprised that staring long and hard at a glass of water failed to turn it into wine. He demanded that Leicester City sell him Peter Shilton. That manoeuvre ended in a firm rebuff, but it was another example of the manager's conceit, his bad manners and rampant ego. The Leicester chairman, Len Shipman, president of the Football League, told me how a meeting of the Foxes' directors was gatecrashed at nine o'clock one evening by the Derby manager, who had simply talked his way into the club, knocked on the boardroom door and barged in to announce: "Gentlemen, I've come to sign Peter Shilton." He received short shrift.

Brian didn't make it home that night. He stayed in the Holiday Inn at Leicester. Nobody could be sure where Shilton was. Shipman phoned me first thing the following morning to complain: "Your manager was totally out of order here last night and I shall be making a formal complaint. I told him in no uncertain terms that I was in the middle of a board meeting, that I had absolutely no intention of discussing Peter Shilton's prospects. I asked him if he would be good enough to leave. Where's Sam? I want a word with him." As luck would have it, Longson was away. Shipman's anger subsided, and the formal complaint never materialised, although Longson inevitably got to hear of yet another incident that damaged his relationship with Clough. Sam loved to rub shoulders with football's power brokers and was left distraught by embarrassing events that made him look weak and foolish.

There was a fascinating scenario with the boys at West Ham when, a month before what turned out to be his final match in charge of Derby County, at Old Trafford, Brian tried to force the issue in pursuit of Bobby Moore and Trevor Brooking. On a previous fishing expedition to London, against the odds, Brian had landed the big one – Dave Mackay, from Tottenham – off the cuff.

Now he was thorough in laying the groundbait for England's World Cup-winning captain, who felt trapped in a deteriorating relationship with Ron Greenwood at Upton Park. Over a boozy lunch at the Churchill Hotel in Portman Square, Moore was guaranteed a huge salary and the promise that he could stay in his family home in Chigwell with his missus, Tina, and need spend only a couple of nights each week in the Midland Hotel – the sort of arrangement that had suited Mackay's lifestyle admirably. Brian and Bobby had a mutual friend in Kenny Lynch, the entertainer, who then chauffeured Moore to Derby for a further meeting during a practice match. The player was still reluctant because he could not visualise himself playing a prominent role in a defence marshalled by Roy McFarland and Colin Todd. At least he was reluctant until Cloughie played his trump card and said: "I'll tell you what I'll do. I'll put you on the pitch and I'll get those two to come up here and watch and learn."

"That was the moment," his old cricket-watching pal Lynch recalls, "that I realised why Cloughie was such a great manager. I looked at Bobby – and he seemed to grow a foot in height."

Brian was confident that he had his man in the bag, and that Brooking would follow. He turned up unannounced at Upton Park, plonked himself down in Greenwood's office and asked for a whisky before announcing: "I've come for Bobby Moore and his mate, Brooking." Brian started talking money, raising the stakes, refusing to take 'no' for an answer. Greenwood refused to sell at any price – even £400,000 – but he promised to put Brian's offer in front of the West Ham board, if only to get him back in his car and up the M1. Greenwood's directors, however, were keen to bank £400,000 for an ageing defender whose glory days were long gone, and a midfield player thrown in, but in a bold act of brinkmanship Greenwood threatened that if Moore and Brooking were allowed to leave, then he would resign and leave the Hammers, who were struggling after an indifferent start to the season, in the lurch. On one hand, Brian came close to pulling off a fantastic double coup for two players who might have made Derby County the best team in England for the second time in three seasons. That's what the fans saw – a brilliant, maverick, breathtaking manager. On the other hand, Brian had torn up the rulebook, employed underhand methods to tap-up Moore, and kept our board of directors in blissful ignorance. When the Derby directors questioned him about the rogue enterprise,

Brian readily accepted that his approach for Moore was illegal, but he did it with a defiant look in his eyes that said: "So what?" He told Sam and myself: "They are quality players, we only want the best to play for Derby County."

* * * * *

The pressure cooker was coming to the boil. It exploded on that Monday, two days after the win at Old Trafford, the day that Brian Clough and Peter Taylor formally handed in their notice – typewritten by Gerald Mortimer, a sportswriter at the *Derby Evening Telegraph* – and it caused a mighty furore in the boardroom where the drinks cabinet remained defiantly out of commission for the morning.

The resignation was the direct result of a fit of temper. It was Clough's way of saying to the world: "I'm the boss; I'm bigger than this club. I'm fed up with the board, I'm fed up with people telling me I can't do this, I can't do that. Look, we're winning matches, look who we are, look how far I've brought this club." Clough thought he had called Sam's bluff and that, whatever the aggro, he would emerge on top with greater power. But what he never appreciated was that his behaviour had pushed Sam over the edge to the point of no return. The chairman had been ground down, humiliated and worn out. He was in his 70s, his sleep was poor and his health was worse. To outsiders, the thought of accepting the resignations must have seemed like swallowing a suicide pill. To Sam, the action was like taking a tablet to cure the biggest headache of his life.

It took next to no time, however, for Brian to realise that he had made a massive miscalculation. Suddenly, the enormity of what he was leaving behind hit him like a slap in the face with a wet towel – a team of champions yet to peak: Roy McFarland, Colin Todd, Kevin Hector, Alan Hinton, Archie Gemmill, David Nish, European Cup semi-finalists, a town full of supporters who worshipped the ground he walked on. Only a fool or a madman would walk away from what he had built, surely? Clough was neither, but genius had deserted him. I'm convinced that he woke up the following morning, asking himself: "What the hell have I done?"

An even bigger mistake was the resignation within 24 hours of Mike Keeling, his great boardroom ally. Keeling was Brian's glorified chauffeur, running around on errands and taking him to matches, and could be relied on to report every cough and spit from the club's inner sanctum back to Clough. Keeling's exit, however noble it looked in support of the manager, was catastrophic for the strategy of the immediate Clough campaign, which was quite simply to reinstate him, a task that spawned a dedicated protest movement. Had Keeling remained in the boardroom, then things might have been very different. With Keeling out of the mix, he didn't know the board's strategy – and that was, of course, to get another manager, a job that fell to me as company secretary.

The Derby fans were outraged by developments; there was a very real sense of loss, and their sense of grievance intensified when Longson came out with a provocative statement. He said: "We will go into the Second Division with our heads in the air rather than win Division One wondering if the club will be expelled from the Football League." Rival chairmen had delighted in getting to Sam and the directors, warning them of the "ultimate sanction" if Brian kept shooting off his mouth. But as for the authorities kicking out one of the Football League's founder members, that sounded ludicrous to supporters. There had never been a precedent.

I spoke to Bobby Robson, the Ipswich Town manager, who I knew and respected, and others I thought might be suitable candidates for a particularly awkward job. But I focused on Dave Mackay, a Rams legend, who was down the road at Nottingham Forest. I succeeded in persuading him to come.

Throughout that period, the protest movement was getting to the players, winding them up to rebel against Dave and stay loyal to Brian. In the middle of the intrigue, Terry Hennessey, the union representative, was a voice of reason. Terry, whose playing career was effectively over after being plagued by injuries to his knees and Achilles tendon, tried to persuade his old teammates not to be too radical, misguided or plain silly. There were one or two players in there who realised what they were doing and tried to get the balance right. They knew that while Brian was the gaffer, as they called him, he wasn't all good, and that their own careers were at risk.

I talked to the FA, I talked to Cliff Lloyd, secretary of the Professional Footballers' Association, and while I struggled to keep the ship afloat there was a home match against Leicester City the week after United. I'd got Gordon Guthrie, the physio, in there. I'd got Jimmy Gordon, the coach. I'd got people who had to keep up morale, and they were coming to me, asking: "What's happening? Is the gaffer coming back? What are we doing?" I had the board coming to me as well, demanding to know: "What's happening? What are we doing?"

I was the guy in the middle of all this, and I was being crucified, the club was being crucified by the supporters and by the media. We had to put a football team on the pitch, we had to go and win a match. The players didn't want to know, didn't want to play, although they were still coming to me, worried that their wages might not be paid. The coaching staff didn't know what to do. Nobody knew what to do. There was I, in the middle, trying to hold the mayhem together. At times it was frightening. Who was going to hold the dressing room together? Who was going to select the team? Gordon Guthrie? He didn't want to be too involved. Jimmy Gordon? He was Brian's second right-hand man after Peter Taylor. But they knew they had a role to play.

It was a bloody mess, and we'd got the full weight of the media coming at us – press, TV, radio. Lights, cameras, action. Shaftesbury Crescent, outside the main entrance, became a feeding frenzy, day in and day out. It was horrendous. The pressure on the morning of the Leicester game was unlike anything I had known professionally. I tried to remain calm, outwardly at least, but on the inside I was a quivering wreck. Everywhere I turned it seemed that every Tom, Dick and Harry wanted to talk to me, wanted to find out what was happening. My office became my bunker, my only sanctuary. What the hell *was* going on? I felt unsure myself. Such was the national interest I even had Members of Parliament calling me for an update. I was surprised that the Pope hadn't called through on a secret line from the Vatican just so he knew where things stood.

During a meeting two days earlier, I'd spelled out the situation to Jimmy and Gordon and the other staff at the club. I'd told them that, despite our various loyalties, we all had a job to do, that we represented the fans, the supporters who paid their hard-earned to watch us play, particularly the season-ticket holders who were there week in, week out, to cheer us on. Our commitment was to them, and all the politics that were playing out in the dressing room and boardroom had to be put to one side. We were all professionals and we needed to act accordingly. I'd felt that it was rousing stuff, but on the Saturday, with the clock ticking down towards kick-off against our East Midlands rivals, I hoped, and prayed, that my call for unity and peace had got through, even if only for 90-odd minutes. In many ways, I'd just been buying time in that meeting, hoping that my words would afford the chairman and his fellow directors some breathing space to work out their next move.

As morning turned to afternoon, my unease grew and I struggled to force down my pre-match sandwiches. Yet for all the scenarios spinning around in my mind, none compared to how the day turned out. We heard via BBC Radio Derby that a big protest march was making its way from the town centre to the Baseball Ground, brass band, banners and all, demanding that Clough and Taylor be reinstated. It was more circus than football match, and shortly before kick-off the showdown that ensued between the two main protagonists in the soap opera engulfing Derby County turned almost to farce.

As the rest of the board filed in shortly before kick-off, feeling very apprehensive about how the players were going to perform after Clough's departure, Sam was already in the directors' box. One of the directors was in tears in my office before the game; he couldn't stand the pressure. "What the hell is going on?" It had become a constant mantra from his mates and he couldn't take much more of it. We were apprehensive about what we were going to get from the crowd. If the players crumbled without their leader, or downed tools out of protest, we'd be done for – it was a powder-keg situation.

And then, just as we were shuffling along the row to our seats, a figure appeared in the B Stand, standing at the entrance closest to the directors' box. They spotted him first from the Pop Side and a great roar went up. Their hero, Brian Clough, was standing statesmanlike, taking the crowd's acclaim. The Ley Stand followed suit and then everyone in the Main Stand was pointing and gasping: "Look who's there. Wow!" Alas, Sam thought the applause was for him and stood up in the directors' box, milking the occasion.

Sensory overload made it seem like only a matter of seconds, but, looking back, Brian stood there like an emperor for something approaching five minutes. Then he disappeared, as in a puff of smoke, and was gone again, as it transpired en route to London for an appearance that night on the *Parkinson* TV show.

Sam Longson recalled the episode in his autobiography, writing:

> *He stood up to receive the acclaim of the crowd – and got what he expected. But the cheers rose again a few moments later when I was urged by those around me to stand up in the directors' box, representative of the board's actions. It was plain to me where the support lay, and despite the fact that 500 or so fans stayed behind after the match to vociferously put their opinions to anyone who would listen outside the ground, there was no doubt in my mind that a*

majority of the supporters had shown by their actions that afternoon that they were backing the board.

I was never sure Sam had seen Brian, and I always suspected that he'd believed all along that the cheers were for him. Either way, one thing I know for sure is that Brian's appearance actually worked in the chairman's favour. It took the sting out of the situation, not just for him but everyone on the board. There was a very good chance that we were going to be pelted by some of the crowd as their anger, frustration and disappointment reached fever pitch, but Brian caught them by surprise and, in the moment he appeared, the whole dynamic of the afternoon changed. The players also played their part, winning the game 2-1, courtesy of goals from John McGovern and Kevin Hector. Theirs was a highly professional job in extraordinarily difficult circumstances.

When Brian followed Peter Taylor down to work at Brighton & Hove Albion at the start of November, and Dave Mackay started to pick up a few decent results, I thought things might improve, but Clough's focus remained fixed on reclaiming "his" job, and he was still messing around with the players. It was sad in a way, tragic almost. He couldn't say goodbye, couldn't let go, even though life had moved on. He may have thought he was a magician, but even he couldn't turn back the sands of time. I wasn't speaking to Brian, not at all. He saw me as one of the board, in cahoots with them. But he should have come to me, and asked: "Can we sort this out? Can we get Sam on board? Can you persuade the board to get it sorted?" Yet he saw me as Sam's man, certainly *with* Sam, and that was it. As far as Clough was concerned, I was the establishment – the enemy.

Even one or two of the players – *his* players – also realised that he was now going too far. They doubted his interference and told him so. Clough, though, thought some of the board members on the fringe were weak and that he could get round them. Men such as Bob Innes, a local estate agent, and Sydney Bradley, the gents' outfitter. They were very upset because they were getting it in the neck from everyone, their business associates and friends. They couldn't stand it. And there was also Bill Rudd, who was a nice man, a solicitor from Swadlincote. None of these guys were hardened professionals in the game like Sam was, or probably I was. They could have been approached and attacked, but the Clough camp didn't realise that I could have been a direct route and conduit to resolving the situation.

Clough should have come and talked to me. We could have sorted it, easy. But he didn't do that. It was his pride, you know. And sometimes he wasn't as savvy as he thought. Everybody, even the playwright Don Shaw, who was a leading light in the protest movement, said he made his big mistake by not embracing me at the time because, whatever he may have thought, there was no threat. Like all our fans, I just wanted the best for the club. I was very supportive of the club, and results on the pitch alone underlined that Brian was good for the club, of course. While making my own stance and position and career within Derby County, I was no threat to him. I didn't want to be the bloody manager. I just wanted to do my job professionally with no interference in issues of corporate responsibility, receipts and money. I had to ensure the club played by the rules and regulations of the Football Association and the Football League. That was my responsibility, one that I took deadly seriously.

Whatever the problems were between Brian and me, looking back I can see that he was always on a collision course with Sam and the board. He wanted total control or he would go. Do I regret standing up to Brian in those days? No. I just regret that there was no stability around him. Had we been able to provide that, then who knows what Derby County could have gone on to achieve? We went to the semi-finals of the European Cup, and if he'd stayed we'd have built on it. Some years later Brian would say that if he had remained at the club, then Derby would have been bigger than Liverpool in the Seventies, that we'd have been one of the top five clubs in England. But I don't believe the era would have allowed him to stay for another 10, 15 or 20 years. He was so successful that one of the big clubs would have come for him, something would have happened and he'd have gone.

At one point I was approached by Liverpool. First Peter Robinson, their club secretary and a good friend of mine, rang me, and then John Smith, the chairman, called. "Would Brian fit the Liverpool style? What's he like?" they both asked. I told them: "What you see is what you get. He's a brilliant manager and what he has done on the field is unbelievable."

Would Brian have succeeded at a big club, an Arsenal, a Manchester United, a Liverpool? I'm not so sure. Look what happened at Leeds. He would succeed anywhere only if it was *his* team; he had to get the rough diamonds and polish them. Unlike the players at Derby had, and those at Nottingham Forest would do, Leeds United's players did not owe their success to him. At Leeds they owed it to Don Revie. Brian always made sure that he sent a magnificent bunch of flowers to a player's wife when she had a baby. It was *his* family. If somebody blinked in the corner of a room then Brian knew about it. He owned players, dominated them, and they loved him for it. But as for players who were already superstars without Brian's help? That was very different.

You might think that he could have tinkered with a big side, signed a striker to take them to the next level, but I don't think that really was his way of doing things. Players had to owe him and he had to own them. He was the Godfather. That's why the players all threatened to go on strike when he left Derby. They'd lost their soul, the head of their family.

I did see Brian a few times after he left Derby County. In fact I did a few business deals with him and we even made a record together, *You Can't Win 'Em All,* on MCA in 1980 with the Canadian singer JJ Barrie, with *It's Only A Game* on the flip side, which made the charts.

But not even Cloughie could win 'em all.

6

Mackay to the Rescue

IN THE grey zone between the trauma of Brian Clough's exit and relief at Dave Mackay's appointment came a moment close to a Whitehall farce. Under siege from rebel players at the Baseball Ground, vice-chairman Jack Kirkland and myself soothed our frazzled nerves with a few glasses of white wine. That was OK – but after three hours I needed a pee. The only option was an empty champagne bucket. Brian Rix would surely have approved.

I ensured that the bucket which came to the rescue later received a thorough cleansing – but Jack and I always knew which one it was because of a dent.

And when Derby County entertained a rival director neither of us particularly liked, I would make a big show out of pouring our visitor a glass of white from a chilled bottle in that bucket. After one very satisfying home victory, Jack said: "We'll have to stop taking the piss, Stuart." It was a little bit of harmless fun while it lasted.

The infamous bucket first came into play while Dave and Des Anderson were still over in Nottingham, Forest playing out a goalless draw against Hull City. At that point, the Derby players decided to submit a letter of mass resignation and refuse to play at West Ham United the following Saturday. They were kicking the door and hammering it with their fists, shouting: "Board out, Clough back. The club's knackered without him."

Had that letter been handed to me, then as general manager I would have been obliged to go the FA, the Football League and the PFA. The consequences were dire for the players, so we didn't want to confront them. We wanted Dave to come through the door at nine o'clock the following morning and declare: "I am the new manager." Then the players' concerns might have been resolved and the club might be able to return to something approaching normality after the circus of the previous fortnight. So Jack and I played for time, waiting for a phone call, wondering: "Where are you, Dave?"

There was a Plan B, to escape out of the back door of the ground and drive to Nottingham to join Dave and Des at the Albany Hotel, but the players were knocking on the boardroom door to hand me their letter. The siege was lifted when they ended their sit-in and left in a convoy of cars for a meeting at Archie Gemmill's house, to plan their strategy to get Clough back. Colin Boulton and Ronnie Webster stayed behind, but Kirkland and myself brushed past their protests as we made a dash for our cars.

Dave's arrival at the club as a player in 1968 had been a masterstroke by Clough. He was the great Dave Mackay, so all the players took to him immediately, but because he'd take them on great nights out they loved him even more. Here was a man who had played alongside and stood shoulder to shoulder with the greats of the era at Tottenham: Danny Blanchflower, Jimmy Greaves, Cliff Jones *et al.* At the time, Derby was the place to be in football. It was all going on around the Midland Hotel, the York Hotel, and Dave was in the middle of it all. He was the king. It all revolved around him. People loved the man and the player. Here was this international star coming from London in this huge left-hand drive American car which he couldn't get into the car park at the Baseball Ground. The size of that motor matched the character of its owner on and off the field. He had his Dave Mackay Club Ties business as well: there was a Manchester United tie, a Liverpool tie, an Arsenal tie, a Spurs tie, of course. And now there was a Derby County tie. On top of that, he'd do Armani ties. Dave was the man. He walked into the dressing room with these shirts and ties from the capital, handed them out to his teammates, and the players loved him for it. He introduced things to the club that these youngsters had never before experienced.

Even old hands like Willie Carlin hadn't known anything like it.

Dave's standing with the players was one of the reasons why I was so confident that he was the man to take over from Clough. He was very straight, very dour when it came to business dealings. He called a spade a spade and was cautious, but always very proper. He got on well with Cloughie when the pair of them were together at Derby, but that drifted a bit when Dave left, perhaps inevitably.

MACKAY TO THE RESCUE

I turned my attention to Dave after an earlier enquiry to Ipswich boss Bobby Robson, who I regarded highly – his brother, Don, lived at Swadlincote and was a regular at the Baseball Ground – was rebuffed. I think Bobby used our interest to get a better deal from the Cobbold family but situations like that happen all the time in business, especially in football.

The next choice was Dave Mackay. He was a leader, idolised by our fans and probably ready for it. He'd been manager at Nottingham Forest for a year, after spending 12 months at Swindon Town, and he ticked the boxes as the ideal candidate to quell any rebellion and take the club further forward. Yet despite his success with us as a player, Dave took some convincing. In fact, he later admitted that he'd considered not taking my call when Ken Smales, the Forest secretary, told him I was on the phone. They were sitting on a coach, ready to travel to a youth team game at Northampton Town, and Dave obviously knew what I wanted to discuss. It was Des Anderson, his assistant, who urged him to take the call and at least listen to what I had to say. "Talk to him, Dave. You can always say 'no'." Thankfully, Dave took Des's advice. As the final whistle blew at the Cobblers' County Ground, Sam Longson, director Sydney Bradley and I walked into the boardroom to ask Forest's chairman, Jim Woolmer, for permission to approach their manager.

Permission was granted and we followed the Forest coach back to Nottingham where a meeting was arranged at the Albany Hotel. Over sandwiches and drinks, Sam explained to Dave what we wanted. In full disclosure, Sam told Dave about the players' revolt but assured Dave that he was the man to take over, and after a brief chat the Scot stood up, walked to the bar where

Anderson was nursing a beer, nodded and told him: "We're going to Derby." Anderson said later: "After only two years in management together we were going to the best team in the land. I was bursting with excitement at the prospect."

Dave appreciated the fabulous opportunity but was adamant that he wouldn't come until he had taken charge of his final fixture for Forest, at home to Hull City. "We have a game on Wednesday and I won't announce I'm coming," he said. He wouldn't budge on that and, obviously, it was a very fraught period. Roy McFarland rang him because the word was out that we were talking to Dave. Roy, who had spent so much time with Dave when they lodged together at the Midland Hotel, told him: "Don't come, there's trouble in the camp here, I wouldn't bother." But Dave was strong. "Look, I'm coming, I'm your new manager. I've got this game but I will be there the day after." And he was as good as his word.

It wasn't easy, though. When Dave came back to Derby there was a period of several weeks when there was still dissent and some of the players gave him and Anderson the silent treatment. Mackay met the players individually, and by the time those meetings were over they all knew exactly his position: "I'm manager, and you'll be treated on merit like everyone else. Now knuckle down or you are away." Still, though, there was resentment within the playing staff, and with the fans' frustrations still bubbling away the board began to wonder if they had made the right decision. It was vice-chairman Jack Kirkland who reassured Sam: "Brian resigned, he has gone. Dave is our manager and we must stick by him."

Kirkland was excellent, and Dave appreciated his support. "Jack Kirkland was a rock," he said. "He refused to yield. He stood up to be counted." So did Dave. He just kept going and going. Training sessions weren't the friendliest of occasions, and prior to that first game against West Ham – a 0-0 draw – he called a team meeting where he told the players: "No matter what you do, Brian is not coming back. He resigned. I can understand why you respect him. I respected him too when I was playing here, but he has gone. Now let's get on with the job."

It was a tricky time and the players were quite strong in their opinions, but Terry Hennessey was exceptional. He was the players' union representative and he got hold of several of them and said: "Hey, we're out of order here, lads." I contacted Cliff Lloyd, the PFA chief executive, and set him straight: "Cliff, there's going to be hell here. Your players are talking about striking." To make matters worse, Brian was meeting the players in a car park at Markeaton Park and fuelling their frustrations. Cloughie, who still believed that he'd be coming back, promised them that would be the case. But it wasn't. Bringing back Brian was never a serious consideration.

The board was adamant that he'd gone and that there had to be life after Clough. Once Dave was in, he was the new manager and that was it. At the end of the year, if he hadn't turned things around, it might have been different, but thankfully things started to improve. After a month the ice had begun to thaw, results were on the up and the dressing room was united once again. Before that, though, it had reached the stage where Dave had confronted one or two of the dissidents and told them: "Look, this is coming to a point where it's you or me. And it's not going to be me because I won't let that happen. I've come in, I've done all this, but you're not responding. Who's the ringleader?

What's it all about?" There were quite a few of them, actually. They all loved Brian. They all loved Dave as well, but Cloughie had given them so much and he was so desperate to get back to Derby and to "his players" that he was pulling them behind the scenes like a master puppeteer, working their wives as well, sending them flowers.

Brian wasn't just playing silly buggers behind the directors' backs, however. He was quite happy doing it to their faces as well, and it led to moments of black farce.

On the day their resignations were accepted by Sam Longson, there was an epic slanging match between the three of them. Brian and Peter were shouting and screaming at Sam, who in turn was yelling back.

Sam: "Get out the bloody door."

Brian and Peter: "No, you get out the bloody door."

It became so petty that Sam demanded they handed back the keys to their company cars there and then. Brian and Peter were shouting: "We'll give you back your bloody car keys but how are we going to get home?" It was a fair question and even in the heat of the battle Sam realised that and relented.

Perhaps unsurprisingly, though, the car keys, let alone the cars, didn't appear back at the Baseball Ground the following day, or the day after that. And when three days had gone by with still no sign of them, I was told to sort it out.

You can imagine the conversation:

Me: "How are we doing with the car, Brian?"

Brian: "Fuck off!"

Me: "How are we doing with the car, Peter?"

Peter: "Fuck off!"

MACKAY TO THE RESCUE

Peter eventually began to come round. "The chairman really wants them back now," I told him, softly, and he was sensible about the situation. He sent someone down with his car, returning it to the club. But not Brian. He was still fuming with Sam. The chairman told me to ramp up the pressure and I was taking advice from the lawyers. Sam said he wanted to get the police involved and there was talk of cancelling the insurance policy so that Brian would be done for driving a car without the proper cover. Unlike with his resignation, this time Cloughie knew just how far to push things and out of the blue I got a call.

"The car's at the Midland Hotel," he growled. "You'll have to pick it up," and down went the phone. I said to Sam: "I think we're all right, I think we've got it now." I dispatched Bob Smith, the groundsman, to the hotel to collect the car, but the next thing I know, my phone is ringing again and it's Bob, calling from the Midland. "Is the car there?" I asked. "Yes, it's at the front door," he said. "But there's no sign of the keys."

I said: "What do you mean? I told you, they will be in reception." But Bob was adamant there was no sign of them. I had to get in my own car and drive to the hotel to find out what was going on. I said to the receptionist: "Brian has told me the keys are with you," but I was met with a blank look. "No, they're not here," she replied. So I had to get back to Cloughie: "Brian, they must have lost the car keys. Who did you give them to – the receptionist? The night porter? Who was it?"

"Fucking none of them," he snapped back. "They're down the fucking drain."

It turned out that, bold as brass, he'd pulled up, switched off the ignition, climbed out of the car, shut the door, locked it, then dropped the keys down the grate right next to where he'd parked. You had to give him his due, he'd got me and the club running around looking for the keys, the girls on reception looking for the keys, everyone basically dancing to his tune. I was embarrassed, absolutely boiling. But the way he did it ... typical Brian Clough – playing us until the very last.

* * * * *

Playwright Don Shaw was vice-president of the protest movement to reinstate Brian Clough as Derby County's manager. These are his candid views:

> *In October 1973, when Clough resigned, Stuart, in my eyes and in those of my fellow pro-Clough supporters, appeared as an evil genie who had enraged Clough to the point that he would not return to Derby while Stuart was still in office. Brian told me that.*
>
> *Many years later, I met Stuart and was impressed by his intelligence and understanding of the affair that had blighted my life and the lives of many other Rams supporters.*
>
> *Stuart was adamant that had Clough stayed, the club would have faced legal action from the authorities. It seemed a good excuse for his behaviour and showed that there are always two sides to any argument.*
>
> *Leicester City was the first home game after Cloughie resigned. I'd met Cloughie at home in Derby and talked to him about coming to the game. I asked him to come to the game and get on a walk around the pitch, and beckon*

the supporters on to the pitch. I said: "They'll all stand by you, facing the directors' box," as they would have, I'm certain of that.

But he said: "No, I might get arrested." He was a strange character, Clough, because on the one hand he was full of all this bravura and certainty and confidence, which he communicated to his team and the supporters and which was one of the reasons why I hated to see him go, because I knew he was a genius. It was obvious.

Instead, of walking on to that famous pitch, he stood in the stand in front of me, about ten feet from the directors' box. It was rather dark in the stand and then Sam Longson, the chairman, stood to take the applause as well. They were both bobbing up and down and you could hardly see them. It was a waste of time and Brian should not have done that.

After my book, Clough's War, I met Stuart in Spain. I had a meal with him, he invited me round to his villa, and I liked him. I understood from his point of view what happened. It's just sad, because he said to me: "If Cloughie had just gone out of his way and confided in me, instead of hectoring and railroading things through, things would have been different."

Brian simply told me, "I wouldn't go back if Stuart Webb was there, I can't stand him."

Stuart was a great business-minded secretary, which is why it was such a great shame, because if Clough had not managed to rile so many people and ruffle so many feathers…

At the turn of the century Cloughie said to me: "I regret resigning from Derby. I should have stayed, even with Stuart Webb there. I should not have resigned because I am absolutely certain that with the one extra player that I needed I'd have taken Derby County on to where I took Nottingham Forest, which was winning two European Cups on the trot. We'd have won it year after year."

Brian's Achilles heel was his mouth.

✱ ✱ ✱ ✱ ✱

Gradually, Dave Mackay and Des Anderson won the players over, Dave's leadership qualities and humour working their magic, along with Des's training schedules. Players who had done well in the sessions would be chosen to play in special one-touch, six-a-side matches on Fridays, and Anderson always reckoned they were the highlight of the week. "Dave always played in them and the length of the final period depended on whether his team was winning or not," he revealed. "If his team was 2-1 down, then play carried on and the whistle was blown as soon as Dave's team equalised."

Anderson was extremely popular in the dressing room but didn't appreciate the humour one day when his poster, bearing the message: "It's a crime to give the ball away," had this added to it in felt-tip pen … "to Des!"

7
Champions Again

O N THE day he walked back into the Baseball Ground, Dave Mackay made no guarantees or promises, but it soon became apparent to me that with the accent on attack, rather than clean sheets, life would still be exciting on the pitch.

As soon as calm was restored, Dave demonstrated his character and his ability as a manager and guided the team to a respectable third-place finish in the First Division in April 1974. I was delighted for Dave – and for the supporters and players – but there was more, much more, to come. Right-back Rod Thomas had become his first signing, and in the February we'd added the driving force of Bruce Rioch, a man who guaranteed a ready source of goals from midfield. Still, Dave wasn't satisfied and in the close season he brought in Francis Lee from Manchester City to supplement our firepower.

It a very shrewd signing and, although Franny was a natural centre-forward, it was a piece of business which went some way to making up for the crushing blow of losing Roy McFarland, our immaculate England centre-half. He wrecked his Achilles tendon in the Home Internationals and I didn't like the look of the plaster cast encasing his left leg. I knew that meant Roy faced months and months out of the game, probably a whole season. As it turned out, local lad Peter Daniel stepped up to partner Colin Todd in central defence. It was as if the description "unsung hero" had been especially coined for Daniel.

The 1974-75 season began slowly, with only one League win from the opening seven games, but results improved significantly in September. In the UEFA Cup, we beat Swiss club Servette 4-1 at Derby and 2-1 in Geneva to set up two epic encounters with Atlético Madrid. Ninety minutes at the Baseball Ground and the same in Madrid produced two 2-2 draws, I was struggling to separate the teams with a cigarette paper as the tie went to the lottery of a dreaded penalty shoot-out. Roger Davies missed his spot-kick, but Capón did us a mighty favour by whacking one over the bar, and the outcome became a matter of sudden death from 12 yards. Archie Gemmill, Henry Newton and 19-year-old Steve Powell held their nerve before Colin Boulton made a wonderful save, hurling himself to his left and turning the 16th penalty of the night, from Eusebio Bejarano Vilaro, on to a post.

The high of beating Atlético provided hope that we might go a long way to burying the memory of Clough's team being cheated out of the European Cup by Juventus in Turin 17 months earlier – but we hadn't reckoned on the powerful home performance of Velez Mostar in what was then still Yugoslavia. In December they overturned a 3-1 defeat at the Baseball Ground to win 5-4 on aggregate. Yet despite that major disappointment, on the home front things were looking up with Dave's Derby playing with a degree of flair we hadn't seen under Clough. We became more dependable at the back, too, despite losing McFarland.

Over Christmas and into the new year, runs of victories were occasionally interspersed by a defeat rather than the other way round and slowly we climbed the table. Liverpool, Ipswich, Everton, Stoke, Sheffield United and Middlesbrough were riding high. By the end of March, with Everton in pole position, we were also right up among the leading pack following successive five-goal sprees against Luton (Roger Davies scored the lot) and Burnley. On Saturday, 9 April, Luton did us a mighty favour by beating Everton 2-1 while Franny Lee's goal against Wolves at home was enough to secure victory and move us two points clear at the top with only three games to go. It was squeaky-bum time again, but now we had players in the squad who had been there before, who knew what it took to win a championship.

Three days after Wolves, West Ham were our next visitors, and victims, seen off by Bruce Rioch's strike, leaving four clubs – ourselves, Liverpool, Everton and Ipswich – still in title contention. On 19 April, we managed only a goalless draw at Leicester, but incredibly our three rivals were all beaten, meaning only one of them – Bobby Robson's Ipswich – could still catch us. We were almost there. I stood for a moment in the directors' box at Filbert Street, soaking in the atmosphere as thousands of travelling Rams fans celebrated in the sunshine. Then I took my broad grin inside to have a quiet drink with the Leicester directors.

We'd booked Baileys nightclub in the centre of Derby for our end-of-season awards bash the following Wednesday, and it seemed as if the whole club was there, players and officials dressed to the nines in dinner jackets. Dave and I had just handed the Player of the Year award to Peter Daniel when word reached us that Ipswich had been held 1-1 at Manchester City. The title was ours. For the second time in four years Derby County were champions of England ... and for the second time in four years we'd clinched it on a day off: first on a Mallorca beach; now in a nightclub. What a script! This time, though, we were together. Realising at the same time, under the same roof, that we'd done it was perfect. Don't get me wrong, it was special the first time, but with Brian in the Scilly Isles while me, Peter and the players were in Mallorca, and the directors were back home, we couldn't celebrate together. This time we could. The party lasted long into the night, several of the players arriving home with the morning milk.

By the time Saturday rolled around for our final fixture, against relegated Carlisle United, I'm pretty certain that one or two of the lads, probably more, had not had a night in all week. But how they deserved it at the end of a demanding campaign – not to mention a long, hard couple of years. The celebrations before the Carlisle game were equally wonderful. I'd arranged for as many of our former stars as possible to be at the Baseball Ground and we introduced them individually as they stepped on to that famous – some would infamous – pitch (the old mud heap on which so much brilliant football had still been played was being dug up and replaced). Some of the greatest names in Derby County's history stood in the centre-circle lapping up the party atmosphere and the acclaim. Then out came the champions to join them, led by Dave Mackay and Des Anderson. The old stars applauded as the lads made their way out, the crowd of

CHAMPIONS AGAIN

36,882 roared and cheered. It was a fitting end to a fabulous season, although as it transpired we might have been better off fielding a team of old boys, given the display that followed in a 0-0 stalemate. It was a hangover of a performance, but I could forgive the team almost anything for the manner in which they had buckled down under Dave's direction and played with style, pride and professionalism.

I don't mind admitting that I enjoyed the 1975 title triumph better than the 1972 version under Brian Clough and Peter Taylor. Having been a goalkeeper, Peter had a fixation with clean sheets and always worked towards that, and their team won the title based on a very strong defence. The dynamic duo's last signing was Henry Newton, a defensive midfielder, from Everton, as if to reiterate the point that they liked solidity at the back – and that was the basis of their success. Dave tweaked the format and made it more attacking, introducing greater flair. Rioch became our leading marksman in 1974-75, with 15 goals from midfield. Franny was a brilliant signing up top, and the pair helped turn Dave's dream of an attacking side into a reality. Dave had played with Jimmy Greaves and Cliff Jones at Tottenham, and he knew how important it was to have attacking players who could thrill a crowd. He gave Derby a side full of flair and attacking genius, a team that got my juices flowing a bit more than Cloughie's had done. It threatened to get even better when Mackay signed Charlie George, another maverick striker, to play in the European Cup the following season.

It is, I admit, a touch ironic, then, that Peter Daniel won our Player of the Year award while Colin Todd was voted PFA Player of the Year. Of course, the bedrock of any attacking side is a solid defence and, even without Roy McFarland until the last four matches, we had one of those.

* * * * *

When he arrived at the Baseball Ground, Francis Lee was past his England prime, but he was still a great entertainer, a terrific footballer and a tenacious little so-and-so into the bargain. Just ask Leeds United's Norman Hunter, whose dust-up with Lee in front of the *Match of the Day* cameras on 1 November 1975 remains one of the most memorable pieces of football footage that the BBC has recorded. The two had "previous" and from the kick-off at the Baseball Ground they were at it again, goading each other, trading insults. When he suspected a hand might have touched his back, Franny went over in the penalty area, somewhere in the region of Norman, and the defender was unimpressed. "What the fuckin' hell are you doing that for?" he barked. The "leg-biter" insisted that Franny had dived into thin air – as he was sometimes prone to do – but the referee, Derek Nippard, saw it differently and awarded Derby a spot-kick from which Charlie George scored.

In the second half all hell broke loose. Looking at the footage now, it doesn't appear that too many blows landed as Franny swung like a windmill, but he ended up with a bloody nose. The warring pair were eventually pulled apart and both sent off, but still it wasn't over and as they trudged off they realised that they were only feet apart, and so everything flared up once more. The Leeds right-back, Paul Reaney, grabbed Mr Nippard's arm, pointing out that it was kicking-off again. Various players piled in to intervene and, eventually, Gordon Guthrie, our physio, got Franny into the dressing room. It was at this point that I suspected I had some urgent work to do. I rarely went down to the dressing room if a player had been sent off – that was strictly a managerial issue – but this was a massive incident and I feared for the repercussions. Remember, it was Derby County and it was Leeds United, one of the biggest rivalries in the country – even if the managers now were Dave Mackay and Jimmy Armfield, rather than the previous protagonists, Brian Clough and Don Revie.

I thought: "Bloody hell, the television cameras are here, everyone is going to see this on the box tonight. And if they're scrapping on the pitch, they'll probably still be scrapping down in the corridor. I'd better get down there." Groundsman Bob Smith was in the dressing room minding his own business and boiling the kettle for a brew when Franny walked in. Gordon followed him through the door and tried to calm him down for a minute or two, before heading back up to the dugout. Gordon was the sponge man and he needed to be ready to go on if anyone got injured – a not unlikely event when Leeds were in town.

Franny was on the treatment table, lying on his back, eyes bulging, absolutely seething. The red mist had descended and you could read his mind. His thoughts were focused on getting to Hunter at any cost. You could see in his face the moment the realisation hit him: the dressing rooms were next to each other and Norman was in the vicinity. Franny was like a great white shark sensing blood in the water. The atmosphere was visceral. Club captain Roy McFarland, who missed the match through injury, also came in to try to settle him down. But for what seemed like an age, Franny was intent on getting to Hunter and finishing what had been started on the pitch. It was sad that the incident had spoilt what was a terrific game of football, settled 3-2 in our favour thanks to a magnificent goal from Roger Davies.

Of course, there were dire consequences for Derby and for Franny, but it led to a rule change that I am convinced has improved football. At that time a player who had been sent off was suspended for the next match, regardless of the competition, which meant that Franny would miss the second leg of our European Cup second-round tie with Real Madrid at the Bernabéu. We had royally thumped Miljan Miljanić's team 4-1 at the Baseball Ground, thanks to a Charlie George hat-trick and David Nish's goal, but the job was far from over. With Franny banned, and Bruce Rioch injured – another sad legacy of the Leeds match – Roy McFarland was pressed into service when less than fully fit. Charlie scored again, giving rise to a fact that I think should become a quiz question: which player scored four goals in a European Cup round and finished on the losing side? I can't think of anyone else but Charlie. We didn't have enough in our locker and lost 5-1 on the night, an agonising 6-5 on aggregate.

Of course, we didn't lose just because we were missing one player, but it was ridiculous that Franny couldn't play in a European tie after being sent off in a domestic game. We lobbied the FA to change the rule so that a player would miss the next match under their jurisdiction – League games, FA Cup matches, League Cup-ties... domestic games, basically, but not European fixtures. The board backed me to push for that change and Derby County drove that paper forward. There was sympathy towards the club within the FA, I think, for what seemed like the first time.

CHAMPIONS AGAIN

Normally, they didn't like change and they certainly didn't like to be questioned on anything, but that one was quite easy because it was understandable; everybody more or less agreed it was a sensible decision. The meeting with the FA passed off smoothly with Ted Croker in charge. We drafted a formal proposal that was seconded and passed, with the new rule introduced the following season.

While Franny missed the trip to Madrid, I certainly didn't and the days leading up to the game will forever remain in my memory. As tradition in European competition dictates, visiting directors and club officials are always welcomed with a lunch. The Real directors were famed for rolling out the welcome mat – more of a red carpet, to be fair – with great style. Two days before the match they invited the chairman and directors to a palace in the city, where we were treated to a lavish banquet that included fresh fish, the tastiest lobsters, washed down with the finest Rioja.

The Spanish hospitality impressed me and I had a thoroughly enjoyable lunch, not least because the club doctor seated to my right was a wonderfully engaging character who regaled me with stories of the greats who had played for his club, tales of Alfredo Di Stefano and Ferenc Puskas and the like. We were enjoying a lively conversation until halfway through the meal when we were interrupted by the unmistakable sound of a helicopter landing outside on manicured lawns. Moments later my companion was approached by a messenger, who whispered in his ear. "Stuart, please excuse me," said my new acquaintance, rising from the table. "As well as being the Real Madrid club doctor, I am also the personal physician of General Franco – and I must leave this instant." It was common knowledge that the General was extremely sick, and two weeks later he died following a heart attack aggravated by peritonitis. Franco had ruled Spain for almost 36 years until two years before his death, and when I think back now to that night, I still feel a sense of history. Many years later I would again feel close to El Caudillo – The Chief – as he was known, because Josie and I bought the house in Marbella which had once belonged to him and where we still live for three or four months of the year. Perhaps Franco was looking down on Real as he neared his own endgame – I've often thought something divine had been needed that night to overturn Derby's lead.

8

A Colourful Cast

SAM LONGSON'S favourite employee, Rene, wore a worried look when she poked her head around my office door to say that there was a gentleman to see me. A gentleman? There was nothing cultured about the appearance of this character – brown trilby, checked suit, straight from the racecourse – who you wouldn't have wanted to meet in a well-lit alley, never mind a dark one, and even less about the punishment he had in mind for the Derby County player who was in debt to his boss, a bookmaker, to the tune of £10,000.

"It's fucking simple," he growled at me. "We get the fucking money, every last fucking penny, by 5pm on Thursday ... or on Friday I'll break his fucking legs."

It was by no means the first time I had fielded a threat like this – mostly it boiled down to chancers trying it on – but now I had a very uneasy feeling that this individual wasn't messing about. The "fun and games" we had with the player in question were never-ending. He was a heavy gambler, but he was also a key member of the team, so we'd prop him up financially every time. And he wasn't the only one frittering away his money – and ours – to be fair. Most of the lads liked a bet, but he took it to extremes that the rest of them never reached. I spoke to Brian about the situation and we realised that this time we had to work fast. We raided a couple of safes around the club, cobbled the cash together, and when the big beast returned on Thursday I handed him a couple of bulging envelopes. In the meantime, we pulled the player to one side and dished out another rollicking, as well as warning him that this was the last time the club would bale him out. We told him in no uncertain terms that he'd be paying us back and, as ever when we'd dug a player out of a financial hole, we ensured that he signed a little slip agreeing to the debt being repaid from his wages.

What didn't help us was the fact Arthur Whittaker's betting shop stood diagonally opposite the main entrance to the Baseball Ground, on the corner of Cambridge Street and Shaftesbury Crescent, next to the chip shop. Arthur had an understanding with the club – little wonder, really, given the custom our lads gave him – and several times he wandered over to have a quiet word with me about clearing a debt. "Look, if you don't sort out this tab, then we are going to have a problem, things could get ugly," was always the gist. He was only a corner shop bookie but I knew that unless I acted promptly, then his boss, based in Birmingham, would make life uncomfortable for all concerned.

We would haul in our unsuccessful gamblers to discover their side of the sorry story and, naturally, their initial response would be a flat denial. They came in looking like startled extras from *Bambi*. Several were young and naïve, and gaining a full confession never over-taxed Brian or myself. "Sorry, boss, it won't happen again. Promise."

Then the stupid sods would wander straight over the road to set up another potentially ruinous tab. Our patience running thin, we discovered the best way to deal with a gambler was to involve his wife. A footballer might be reduced to tears by Brian Clough, but he was always more afraid of his own missus. She would come in to my office with her husband to learn the full extent of his debt. Then, after the initial shock, she bristled with indignation, glancing sideways with a look that said: "Just you bloody well wait until I get you back home!" Those characters were always more successful in the three o'clock at the Baseball Ground than they ever were in the two-thirty at Haydock Park.

Of course, everyone has their vices and in a small town, as it was then, such as Derby, it's difficult to keep the lid on things. I received occasional letters from local girls claiming that "so and so has got me in the club," and she wouldn't be talking about the guest list at Tiffany's. It was another headache we needed to solve – and quickly. One such letter informed us that a Derby County player had got a young lady pregnant and that if it didn't get sorted, she would throw herself under a Trent bus. I recall the club paid some money to make that particular problem go away. But what else do you do in that situation? It was local, right on our doorstep, it was raw, and we had to find a solution.

* * * * *

One lady who made our lives considerably easier was Rene, a wonderful woman in charge of the kitchen at the Baseball Ground. She fussed over the chairman and me like a mother hen. Our daily routine tended to be uncomplicated. Sam drove down from his home in the hills of Chapel-en-le-Frith in north Derbyshire, arriving in my office around 11.30am to spend maybe an hour with me and sign a few cheques as we worked our way through any other business. Brian Clough made his entrance about 12.30pm following his main business of the day, training, after which he and Sam would talk. They were the happy days, when life was sweet and the results suggested that anything was possible.

When he entered my office on those mornings, Sam was often still wearing his big, long overcoat, a trilby perched on his head, and chugging on a cigar, like Winston Churchill. In fact, he thought he was Derby County's "Churchill", did Sam. He was certainly the main man around the Baseball Ground – whatever Brian Clough might have thought. On arrival at the ground, Sam helped himself to a large brandy, a huge slug, and drank half of it in a single swallow. He topped up the remainder with lemonade to concoct a "brandy shandy" that he then sipped throughout the day, carrying it with him along the corridor for his chats with Brian and making it last until it was time to disappear back into the countryside. I never quite worked out whether he found it some sort of comfort, but he certainly needed that brandy and a splash when life turned sour with Brian. Remy Martin was Sam's favourite tipple. Most football clubs had that brand in their boardroom and there was always a warm welcome for him on our travels around the country.

Sam sat himself down opposite me, puffing away at his cigar, and, within seconds, Rene appeared, having clambered over assorted boxes of fish and sacks of potatoes left for Brian and

A COLOURFUL CAST

Peter by adoring fans – but I never once saw her spill a drop of the coffee she percolated for Sam or drop the plate of hot-buttered toast on the tray perched on one hand. Coffee, toast, Remy Martin and a cigar … Sam was set up for the day. He loved his toast, which Rene cut into little fingers for him. He might have been a self-made millionaire with a lucrative haulage business but the chairman was, at heart, an honest, down-to-earth Derbyshire lad with simple tastes.

Sweeping down from his home in his big Rolls-Royce, he licked his lips at the prospect of the Baseball Ground toast. Sam was a very smart dresser, a proper old-fashion gentleman, and I sighed inwardly at the sight of the butter dripping off his toast on to a beautiful silk club tie together with cigar ash. He might have been in a greasy spoon café … or a *Monty Python* sketch. He had been in my office for only five minutes but he looked a wreck by the time he had polished off seven or eight soldiers. Rene looked at him in despair – much like a mum after a messy breakfast in charge of a scruffy, unkempt schoolboy – and tried to pat him down while Sam wriggled this way and that because he was more interested in drinking his coffee and talking through the day's business with me. By the time Sam left, the cheques were invariably butter-stained. Shambolic, but that was Sam: unpretentious, and people loved him for it. Rene, especially, leaving him a tea cloth to dab at the oily stains and ash on his tie and suit.

The respect between Sam and I was mutual, and in his autobiography he was effusive in his praise. He wrote: *"From the moment Stuart Webb took over the position it was apparent that he was a brilliant secretary who had a lot to contribute to the club. He was the kind of man we had been seeking for years. He went on to polish our administration to the highest possible level."*

Sam might not have been the man who first hired me, but in no time at all he showed that he would stand shoulder-to-shoulder with me when the man who did give me the job called it on.

"When I got to know Stuart," Sam continued, "I was surprised that Brian had taken on a young man who obviously had such a mind of his own and was not prepared to be just a 'yes' man to the management. It wasn't long before there was trouble, as he and Brian had their differences.

"During the months to come, Brian repeatedly implored me to sack Stuart. At one time he even went as far as to say that if the secretary stayed, he would go."

✱ ✱ ✱ ✱ ✱

Rene starred in a cast of wonderful characters who made the Baseball Ground a fantastic place to work. Supporters tend to think only of the players and the managers, and occasionally more prominent members of a club's hierarchy. But behind the scenes there are always the unsung heroes. Bob Smith was one, the senior groundsman who famously appeared with a bucket of whitewash and a tape measure to solve the problem of the missing penalty spot during a game against Manchester City at the Baseball Ground in April 1977, an incident featured on *Match of the Day*. Bob had joined the club ten years earlier and was famously told by Cloughie upon his arrival that he'd be doing well if there was still any grass on that famous old pitch at the end of his first month.

A COLOURFUL CAST

In those days groundsmen and odd job men might be recruited from almost off the street. They would happen to be passing and Brian would call out, "Can you cut grass?"

"Well, yeah," they'd reply.

"Can you paint?"

"I suppose so."

"Right, well get up to my house and grab a brush." He'd have them working on the ground in the morning and at his home in Allestree in the afternoon. He had the apprentices at it as well, driven up by the busload to clear the autumn leaves from his driveway. To begin with, no one batted an eyelid. It was character-building for the youths, and saved Brian a heap of work and money.

Sam thought it was quite funny until things got nasty at the end. And then all Brian's non-football enterprises were used as a stick to beat him with.

Cloughie signed groundsmen as well as players, I left him to it, and often I'd know someone was employed only after I'd seen them in the corridors at the Baseball Ground three or four days running. On one occasion I bumped into a chap dressed in overalls who smiled at me.

"Are you an outside contractor?" I asked.

"No," he grinned, "I'm the club's new electrician and maintenance man, my name's Barrie Clough. Has our Brian not told you?"

No advertisement, no interview, no discussion about security, terms or a contract. Just create a job and keep it in the family. Fantastic – as long as you weren't the one who had to try to accommodate Brian's brother into the wages budget.

At times it seemed like an open house, an asylum. Nowadays, security at top clubs' stadiums and training grounds is very tight, but in Brian Clough's time at the Baseball Ground there was always someone wandering around. Often it was a football writer eager to have a chat with the manager, the players, even the groundsman, to discover what was happening behind the scenes.

Brian and Peter were always the main source but they all fed stories to reporters, and so Derby was a happy hunting ground for the press pack.

Respected journalists such as John Sadler of *The Sun* and Ray Matts of the *Daily Mail* were trusted and I enjoyed an excellent working relationship with them as well as with the local boys. I got on with all the press lads, I'd play golf with them, go out drinking with them on tour.

Yet scarcely a week seemed to pass without me answering a torrent of calls: "Is it true Brian and Peter are off to Barcelona?" … "Coventry want them; what's the score, Stuart?" Name a top club and at some point those two were invariably linked with them. Emergency board meetings were called because there were reports that they were going to Madrid, or flying to Barcelona. Clough and Taylor leaked word of a club's interest, and whether it was genuine, or manufactured by the pair themselves for their own reasons, I'd be fending off the press.

Brian was pure gold for the media. They loved him. He filled the column inches for them. But the situation became an uncontrollable monster. Brian also used the press to tap up players he fancied. He and Peter were good at that; they knew how to work the system. In the meantime, they left me fighting

A COLOURFUL CAST

so many fires lit by our management team that I considered changing my name to Red Adair.

* * * * *

In March 1975, midfield star Bruce Rioch and I made headline news in both the local and national press when we were summoned to Number 10 Downing Street by Harold Wilson's staff. As Football League champions, Derby County were among a number of organisations lobbying the Government for VAT to be reduced in sport, and as members of the Central Council of Physical Recreation we were invited to the Prime Minister's residence to make a case on behalf of football. England cricketer Colin Cowdrey, athlete Mary Peters, who won pentathlon gold at the 1972 Olympic Games in Munich, and England rugby union star Andy Ripley also tried to convince the Prime Minister that 100 per cent VAT relief ought to be introduced to release money for local sports clubs to spend on improving facilities.

We wanted to take a player with us, and Bruce was the best man for the job, very articulate and capable of holding his own in any company. We had a fantastic day. I'm sure that Huddersfield Town supporter Harold might have made things a little harder for me had I told him that I hadn't voted for him, but I kept my own counsel on that one. Number 10 was seriously impressive with that giant staircase, trodden by some of history's most powerful figures, right before us as we stepped through the front door. I half expected to see a picture of Cloughie hanging from the wall above it, alongside those of every past PM, but, try as we might, neither Bruce nor I could find it. We were led into a little ante room where Bruce and I delivered our speeches. We spent about

20 minutes addressing the PM and his advisers, who included the Sports Minister, Denis Howell, a former Football League referee, explaining why the tax break would be so beneficial.

I suspected that Bruce had the drive, intelligence and personality to become a first-class manager. His success at Middlesbrough, winning two promotions, and Bolton, where he won another promotion and took the Trotters to the League Cup Final, did not surprise me in the slightest, but he got a bit stuffed at Arsenal. He was in charge there when Dennis Bergkamp was signed but the players at Highbury failed to support him and Bruce made way eventually for Arsene Wenger. He had a lot to offer. His father was a military man so he had that background and always carried himself well, in a correct and proper manner. Bruce was never afraid to express his opinion, and that's perhaps why it didn't work for him as a boss. Maybe he needed to mellow a touch. But as a player he was top class, a great, and during his time at Derby County he was fantastic.

Alan Durban was another who I thought would make a good manager, and he enjoyed a decent career in the hot seats at Stoke, Sunderland and Cardiff. Cloughie mocked Alan because he always had a lot to say, although I always liked that about him and, secretly, Brian did too.

Alan Hinton was quality with an excellent media presence. It was no surprise to me that he went over the Atlantic to carve out a big reputation for himself with Vancouver Whitecaps and Seattle Sounders. Commercially astute, Ally was the first player to wear those distinctive white boots that he made famous. Or was he? There is a photograph of that great Rams figure, Steve Bloomer, wearing white boots back in the 19th century. *Plus ça change* …

A COLOURFUL CAST

Archie Gemmill dabbled on the fringes of club management without ever quite making the step up, although he did enjoy some stunning success as a coach under Clough at Nottingham Forest.

Roy McFarland hankered after management but, like Colin Todd, when he became a boss he tended to live on his reputation as player, and I didn't think that really worked for him. Take nothing away from Roy: as a number-two to Arthur Cox, he was fantastic.

Of them all, though, it was Dave Mackay who was cut out to succeed as a manager and, sure enough, our decision to appoint him in the wake of the Clough turmoil proved to be a masterstroke.

9

Thrill of the Chase

Dave Mackay was by no means as volatile as his predecessor – but the thrill of the chase was still very much in evidence when he set out to sign a couple of exciting, big-name stars for Derby County.

Dave had already experienced disappointment in his quest to bring another proven goalscorer to the Baseball Ground. In March 1974, he had a long face when he returned from a trip to the Hyde Park Hotel where he'd failed to persuade Peter Osgood to join Derby, and then watched the Chelsea centre-forward slip away to Lawrie McMenemy's Southampton.

Days before the start of the 1974-75 season, word reached us that 30-year-old Francis Lee might be available for £100,000 at Manchester City, where manager Tony Book considered that the player's best days were behind him. Age meant nothing to Mackay, though, and he reminded me of how his move to Derby at veteran status had rejuvenated his career. In his opinion, Franny guaranteed class and quality, and could add to the medals

THRILL OF THE CHASE

he had won at Maine Road. "We've got to get up to Manchester as soon as possible, Stuart, and talk to Franny," he said. But would Lee come to Derby? Well, we'd just got into Europe and felt that was the ace up our sleeve.

We arrived at a restaurant near Franny's mansion in Wilmslow, and in he swaggered, very suave. He had been all round the game: the World Cup with England in 1970; titles and cups with City – Franny had done it. He'd read the book, printed his own T-shirt. He owned racehorses and ran a profitable paper manufacturing business. He had everything. There wasn't much you could tell – or sell to – Francis Lee.

He was the man and greeted us with a cheery: "What's it all about, boys?" Over a fine bottle of white wine the three of us quickly cut to the chase. Money was no problem, but he still wanted to think about the offer. Then a waiter approached and said: "There's a telephone call for Mr Lee." Franny made his excuses and went to reception, leaving Dave and myself frowning at each other. We read each other's minds: someone else had come in for him; someone else was knocking on the door. Our fears were confirmed when Franny returned to the table to inform us that, as attractive as it was, he definitely wanted to sleep on Derby's proposal.

As Franny pushed back his chair, sipped his coffee, chewed his lip and gazed out of the window, Dave and I went to the gents where I told the manager: "If we don't do the deal tonight, we're fucked. We're going to lose him."

Dave tried to reassure me: "Relax, Stuart. He'll be alright. Franny and I go back years and years, there's a lot of respect between us."

"No, Dave," I said. "We've got to do it, and we've got to do it right now."

We went back to the table and, pulse racing, I spoke quickly: "Look, we're qualified for Europe and if we don't get this deal signed now, then we'll miss the deadline for nominating you in our squad for next season's UEFA Cup. There are some cracking teams in there too – Real Madrid, Ajax, Inter Milan, Juventus. We have to submit our list of eligible players in the next 48 hours. You're our first choice, Franny. You know you are, otherwise we wouldn't have driven up here to have this conversation. But Dave wants to buy another centre-forward and we'll have to move on quickly if you don't sign."

Franny looked at us in turn, smiled, stuck out a hand and said: "Done." In some respects, he rather had been. Not that he ever regretted that decision.

European football was the big carrot for Franny, something City could not offer. Our opposition that lunchtime was none other than Tommy Docherty, who I discovered was offering him the world to sign for Manchester United and help them escape the Second Division at the first time of asking, a feat they managed without Franny's assistance.

Months later, Franny came to see me at the Baseball Ground for a chat. We discussed business and just as he was leaving, he said: "Oh, by the way, you know when you told me when I signed about that date for European eligibility, did you get your dates wrong?"

"No, I don't think so, Franny," I lied.

"It's just that I've found out that the list didn't have to be in to UEFA until a fortnight after our lunch!"

THRILL OF THE CHASE

Franny became a typical Dave Mackay player, a great character and a very good signing. He loved Derby, met his wife there and the fans loved him. In fact, they adored him after he weighed in with a dozen goals to add another First Division champions medal to his impressive collection of silverware. I have since met Franny several times in Barbados and enjoyed playing golf with him. Still a top man!

Franny Lee's goals helped Derby County win the First Division again in 1974-75, but the chances of Mackay resting on his laurels were nil. The European Cup became his Holy Grail as he set out to emulate his fellow Scots, Jock Stein at Celtic and Matt Busby at Manchester United, and win the trophy with the big ears. When he got wind that Charlie George – darling of Highbury's North Bank – had reached the end of his tether with Bertie Mee and was determined to leave Arsenal, Dave wanted him.

But in July 1975, the Rams manager was on holiday in Edinburgh when a journalist in London tipped me off that Charlie was leaving Arsenal to go to Tottenham for £100,000. I relayed the bad news to Mackay, who said: "Oh Christ, he's not, is he?"

I confirmed what I knew, and Dave told me to stall Charlie while we flew to London to talk to him personally. I contacted Arsenal, who accepted our offer to match Tottenham's £100,000, before I spoke to Charlie, telling him that in two months' time he could be playing in the European Cup with us. "Dave and I will meet you in London tomorrow," I said.

He was interested but said mournfully: "It's almost all done this end, mate. I'm at Spurs for the press conference at midday tomorrow."

Terry Neill, the Tottenham manager, made a huge mistake that day. Everything was in place for him to complete the transfer but he was keen to stage-manage the business and show off Charlie to the media. After all, he was taking him from Spurs' fiercest rivals. I was convinced that Dave's dash to Heathrow would be in vain. However, the following morning as I was about to take our daughter, Beverley, to school – we were in the car, pulling out of the drive – Josie came running out of the house to tell me: "There's a man on the phone, asking for you. Don't ask me who it is, I don't know. I can't understand him!"

I went inside, picked up the receiver and heard Charlie George say: "Are you lot fackin' camming? Are we fackin' on, or what?"

I took a deep breath and replied: "Charlie, we are most very definitely on. We are coming, we're on our way down. Dave and I are both coming. We'll see you at the Hilton Hotel at twelve o'clock.

Charlie spluttered: "I can't be there. There's a press conference at White Hart Lane."

"Forget Spurs," I insisted. "Just be there at twelve o'clock and we'll close the deal. The phone went dead with Charlie's immortal words: "Diamond geezer." Dave was already at the Hilton Hotel in Park Lane, and we had a few nervous few minutes before Charlie walked in and quickly signed a contract. While we celebrated Dave's capture of another great player with a round of drinks at the bar, at White Hart Lane the name "Charlie George" was written on a pad on a table in front of an empty chair.

One of Islington's finest natural talents had been reared on playground tales of Dave Mackay's swashbuckling feats at the other end of the Seven Sisters Road, and he signed for us

THRILL OF THE CHASE

because it was Dave's champions – the team, the success, the attraction of what we were doing, and the lure of Europe. All those things added up to a huge incentive. Finally, Charlie was North London through and through, so he was a bit twitchy about Tottenham and how that would go down with his Arsenal-supporting mates.

Neither Franny Lee nor Charlie George came cheap in terms of wages, although the £100,000 transfer fees we paid fell into the bargain category. Influential characters within the game were intrigued about how little Derby could compete financially with the biggest clubs in England. When Manchester United were in the Midlands, Sam Longson and I would often bump into Matt Busby, United manager turned director, at the Mackworth Hotel. One day, he enquired: "How come you won the title with gates of 30,000, and we get 60,000 at Old Trafford? Is Sam putting in the money? Are the directors putting money in?"

No, Derby competed at the highest level because we were extremely cute, if not the best, when it came to utilising sponsorship – and that's where I played a significant role, establishing a stream of profitable commercial activities. Texaco were persuaded to pay £30,000 for exclusive advertising rights on the Baseball Ground while sponsors were courted for every home match we played, and they paid what they could afford.

As I have already said, I introduced *The Ram*, the club's newspaper, which sold twice as many copies at newsagents as it did on a match day doubling as a programme. We established 16 supporters' national and international branches, taking coachloads of fans home and away, and I set up the Junior Rams club specifically to cater for the next generation. With money, you can get talented players, so we had that little edge. And Brian Clough and Dave Mackay weren't just good managers, they were outstanding at their jobs.

While Arsenal fans of a certain vintage have vivid memories of Charlie George scoring an FA Cup winner against Liverpool at Wembley in 1971, and promptly celebrating by lying flat on his back, Derby supporters were treated to something equally spectacular when Real Madrid came calling in the European Cup in October 1975, and were left licking their wounds from a 4-1 defeat after Charlie scored a wonderful a hat-trick, which included two penalties.

Charlie scored a blinder again in the return leg but, crucially, we badly missed the injured Bruce Rioch, and Franny Lee who was suspended as a result of his infamous fight with Leeds United's Norman Hunter. Real, of course, overturned the odds in Madrid to win 6-5 on aggregate.

But it was Charlie's three goals at the Baseball Ground that prompted a crazy case of mistaken identity. Club Brugge president Dr Michel D'Hooghe, now a FIFA Ex-Co member, told me: "We'd like to buy your big centre-forward, the number-nine."

Now Charlie wore our number-11 shirt, Franny wore nine and, although he had a massive heart, at 5ft 8in there was no way that he could be described as big in terms of height. So with Franny suspended in Madrid, Roger Davies was our big centre-forward, the number-nine. Of course, in those days there were no squad numbers. Players swapped shirt numbers depending on what position they were playing.

"Yes, he's available," I told the Belgian club. "The price is £400,000."

THRILL OF THE CHASE

Roger had joined the Rams from Worcester City for £15,000 – plus a box of fruit from Sam Longson who, apart from his haulage business, came from a farming background in North Derbyshire and against the odds, had made a commercial success out of growing raspberries in the Peak District. That's the way football men could behave. I might negotiate a modest deal and into the mix toss a case of wine, and we'd shake on it. That little extra sweetens the deal nicely, makes you feel good. It's something a little more personal than a cheque or a banker's draft.

By the end of the season, Mackay had accepted that Derby were in a position to turn a handsome profit on Roger Davies, and he was looking to reinvest after Franny retired and Alan Hinton departed to America for a fresh challenge in the North American Soccer League.

Alan's replacement was already at the club, Dave having splashed out a club-record £310,000 to take Leighton James from Burnley, but the Welsh international flattered to deceive and rarely suggested that he could integrate successfully.

Roger and I went over, saw the Club Brugge board and chatted. They were looking forward to a run of their own in the European Cup and offered Roger a tidy increase on his salary. He had served the club faithfully, enjoyed several purple patches when it came to goals, yet had often suffered as a reserve when at other First Division clubs he would have been an automatic choice. On the flight home, I wanted to be sure he wasn't leaving us with any sense of regret. "Are you happy, Roger, with all of the terms they've offered?" He smiled and said: "Yes, very happy."

When Roger returned to Belgium to start pre-season training, the Club Brugge head coach, Ernst Happel – one of the greatest managers in the history of the game – took one look at him sitting expectantly in the dressing room and enquired gently: "Excuse me, but who are you?" Roger replied: "I'm the number-nine from Derby you wanted."

Happel went ballistic: "Like fuck you are! I wanted the centre-forward who scored the hat-trick against Real Madrid." The confusion had arisen because Happel had seen the Derby-Real match, seen Charlie George excel, and gone to his board and the club's general manager, telling them: "That's who I want, the Derby centre-forward." When Roger and I did the deal, it was in the summer, and Happel wasn't around. The first time the head coach saw him was when he turned up for pre-season training. The Belgians were not prepared to pay £400,000 for Roger Davies, so we compromised on a figure of £135,000, but he became quite a favourite over there, helping them to a domestic league and cup double, and winning the Belgian player of the year award. Roger got his break and played well in couple of European games, scoring a penalty to help knock Panathinaikos out of the European Cup.

Face in the crowd: where I began my lifelong passion for football, in the Deepdale crowd, watching the great Tom Finney.

The new boy: 1 June 1970, and my first day as secretary of Derby County, flanked by Rams chairman Sydney Bradley (left) and vice-chairman Sam Longson, the real power in the boardroom, soon to take over from Bradley.

Early edition: one of my first innovations, in 1971, was the launch of the club newspaper, The Ram. *From left to right: Sam Longson, me, Peter Taylor, Mike Keeling and Brian Clough.*

Disappearing act: two apprehensive characters flank Ian Storey-Moore as he is introduced as Derby's "new signing" before a game against Wolves in March 1972. Brian Clough remained in the dressing-room, leaving Peter Taylor and me out on a limb.

Champions! May 1972, and players and staff returned from Mallorca to receive the League championship trophy at the Baseball Ground, which was specially opened on a Sunday morning so that tens of thousands of fans could salute their heroes.

At Derby's Council House with Sam Longson, Brian Clough and the Mayor of Derby, Joe Carty, who presented Sam with a silver bowl to mark the Rams' League championship win.

Trophy wives: Rams wives parade the trophy as Brian Clough, Peter Taylor, me, Sam Longson and Jimmy Gordon take a back seat.

With Sam Longson and Colin Todd at the PFA Player of the Year dinner. Toddy got to London, took out his dress shirt, then realised that it needed cufflinks. He ended up wearing Tom Pendry's. Lord Tom has often reminded me that he never got them back.

On the Baseball Ground pitch, Brian and Peter put pen to paper on a new deal. Interestingly, Sam doesn't have his hand on Brian's shoulder, but on Peter's. I'm sure that things had started going wrong between them by that point.

Derby County's manager is prepared for the camera, watched by ITV commentator Brian Moore. High-profile Cloughie's provocative opinions were now embarrassing Sam Longson and his board.

October 1973 and a grim-looking Clough and Taylor have handed in their resignations. The board has accepted them, unleashing a storm of protest from players and supporters alike.

Outside the Baseball Ground, Alan Hinton does his Neville Chamberlain impression. Colin Boulton and Ron Webster smile for the camera. The players were campaigning to have Clough and Taylor reinstated.

Bailey's nightclub in May 1975 and another championship celebration: left to right of the back row are Trevor East, Alan Durban, and Sam Longson; front row shows Frank Cholerton, Dave Mackay and me.

New Rams boss Dave Mackay makes the key signing of Bruce Rioch from Aston Villa. Dave took over in difficult circumstances, rode the storm, and produced another championship-winning team.

Together with Dave Mackay, acknowledging the Baseball Ground fans after Derby County won the title for the second time in four seasons.

The League championship trophy sits on the centre-spot at the Baseball Ground as players old and new join hands to sing Auld Lang Syne. From left to right are yours truly, Peter Daniel, Harry Bedford, Jim Bullions, Jack Webb, Steve Powell, Ronnie Webster, Willie Carlin, Terry Hennessey, Reg Matthews, Reg Ryan, Johnny Morris, Bill Townsend, Peter Docherty and Jack Parr.

The Riverside Hotel for Peter Daniel's testimonial with Dave Mackay and Bill Shankly. Shanks didn't want to come, as you can probably tell by his expression, but I persuaded him to come as guest speaker and he was brilliant.

Stars of stage, screen and sport. From left to right are Bobby Moore, Jimmy Tarbuck and Eric Morecambe next to me.

Rubbing shoulders with royalty: HRH The Duke of Edinburgh chats to Sam Longson.

The Derby County secretary poses proudly with the Football League championship trophy and the FA Charity Shield.

Chatsworth House on the eve of the 1976 FA Cup semi-final at Hillsborough. The Duke of Devonshire invited us for a cup of tea and a walk around the grounds before we made our way to the team hotel in Sheffield.

Francis Lee and Charlie George in conversation before training at Raynesway. Both men are in my Derby County "All-star" team.

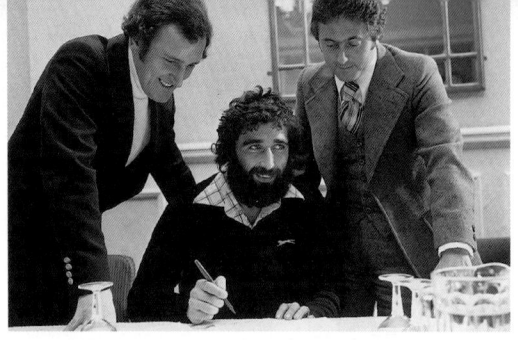

Colin Murphy is pleased to see Derek Hales sign on the dotted line. But Hales proved an expensive flop at the Baseball Ground.

February 1977: Barrie Eccleston of BBC Radio Derby talks to Cloughie on the day he came to the Baseball Ground to say he wasn't returning to manage Derby County. Two days earlier, Cloughie had met George Hardy (standing next to Eccleston) and me at the Riverside Hotel to discuss an offer. He went away, slept on it, got a better deal at the City Ground, and then told us: "I couldn't leave Forest. I've just painted Nigel's rabbit hutch red."

Dave Mackay, Nobby Stiles and Mike Summerbee, and John Prescott, a future Deputy Prime Minister, are some of my teammates in the charity match organised by Tom Pendry.

I've just nutmegged Tommy Docherty. Honestly ... !

I watch Tom Pendry MP blast a penalty in a charity match. To Tom's dismay a goal was disallowed when the ref ruled that the ball hadn't touched the goalkeeper before Tom put the rebound into the net. To my right is Dave Mackay, while Tommy Docherty is the United player nearest the camera.

The Doc: Tommy Docherty came to Derby at the end of his managerial career and tried to change the squad by selling far too many established players and replacing them with inferior signings. It wasn't his best spell in management.

Judith Hann – the longest-serving presenter on BBC TV's Tomorrow's World *and daughter of former Derby player and trainer Ralph Hann – interviews me. She did a current affairs show called* The Risk Business *about football and in 1980 came to talk to me about the success of Derby County off the field, our sponsorship, all the innovations we were introducing at the time.*

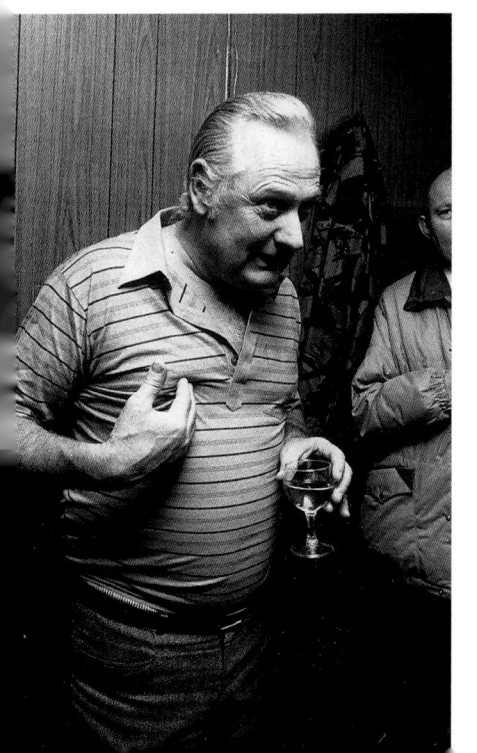

Peter Taylor is happy – the Rams have just beaten Nottingham Forest in a memorable FA Cup tie at the Baseball Ground – but eventually Peter couldn't keep Derby County out of Division Three.

April 1984, and I chair my first Derby County board meeting. From left to right are Colin McKerrow, John Kirkland, me, Chris Charlton, Fred Fearn, Bill Hart and Trevor East.

An embrace from a great Rams servant. Gordon Guthrie served under every Derby County manager since the legendary Harry Storer in the 1950s right into the 21st century. Gordon has seen it all – what a book he could write!

All smiles as I pose with new Rams manager, Arthur Cox. Arthur did well for us in his early days, taking the club back to the old First Division from the Third.

With Ian Maxwell, who Captain Bob insisted took over from me as chairman. Club solicitor Arthur Willis is to my right.

Celebrating promotion from Division Three in May 1986 with some young supporters on the Baseball Ground pitch.

Toasting promotion to the First Division with Roy McFarland and Arthur Cox.

With Peter Shilton, our "£1million signing" – at least that was how Robert Maxwell wanted to spin it.

Sitting with Robert Maxwell at a Baseball Ground press conference after Captain Bob assumed the chair following the Rams' promotion. He didn't want his son to be chairman of a club higher up the Football League than the one he was leading.

Shilton's Southampton and England teammate Mark Wright also signed. He is pictured here with Arthur Cox, Robert Maxwell and me. Despite his smile, Captain Bob was less than keen.

Another top signing: Dean Saunders joins the Rams for £1million in October 1988. Arthur Cox and me look on.

Family affair: Robert Maxwell sweeps into Derby County. Outgoing chairman Ian Maxwell leads the way.

Ironic words from one Rams fan impressed by Maxwell's apparent investment in Derby County's future.

The Maxwell helicopter hovers over the Baseball Ground. In fact, the Derby County chairman was hardly ever seen at a match.

Robert Maxwell parades his Czech "signings" for Derby County. It turned out to be another one of Maxwell's elaborate schemes.

What a difference a year makes! By now, Rams supporters had grown tired of Maxwell's lack of interest in their club.

The toughest interview of my life! I am grilled by my daughter Beverley, who was then a sports journalist and presenter for Sky Television.

With Bobby Robson, who was probably explaining to me why he didn't come to Derby. I'm certain Bobby used my interest in hiring him to get himself a new deal from the Cobbold family at Ipswich Town. And who could blame him? He was England manager by this time when he came to a Derby match.

Receiving an award from Lord Aberdare, chairman of the Football Trust Community Award Scheme, on behalf of Derby County. Getting the club involved in the local community was always one of my priorities.

Getting away from it all. Josie and me are relaxing at our home at Longford Mill with some of our family pets. We loved our time in Derbyshire.

I'm not sure why we all looked so glum! Maybe new manager Jim Smith has just been advised of his transfer budget. With Rams owner Lionel Pickering and the Bald Eagle in the summer of 1995. Twelve months later we were celebrating promotion to the Premiership.

With daughter Beverley, savouring the unique atmosphere at the Baseball Ground on 28 April 1996 — the day Derby County returned to the top flight.

Chairman and owner of Derby County, Lionel Pickering, acknowledges the applause of grateful Rams fans as their team rejoin the elite of British football.

Dancing for joy! Lionel does a lap of honour as I acknowledge the crowd and John Kirkland is about to throw his hat to the fans.

Captain Marvel! I celebrate with Dutchman Robin van der Laan, whose header sent the Rams back to the top flight with a 2-1 won over Crystal Palace on 28 April 1996.

What an occasion ... I drink in the moment of victory over Crystal Palace and promotion to the Premiership. Derby County are going back to the top. What a way to celebrate 25 years with the club!

As chairman, launching the World Series, a vehicle for top football clubs to spread their brand globally in the Middle East, India, China and North America.

Congratulating AC Milan's Umberto Gandini on winning the inaugural Dubai Soccer Challenge.

In Dubai with the great Brazilian footballer Romario, then manager of Vasco da Gama, and now a politician.

*With the World
Series Cup.*

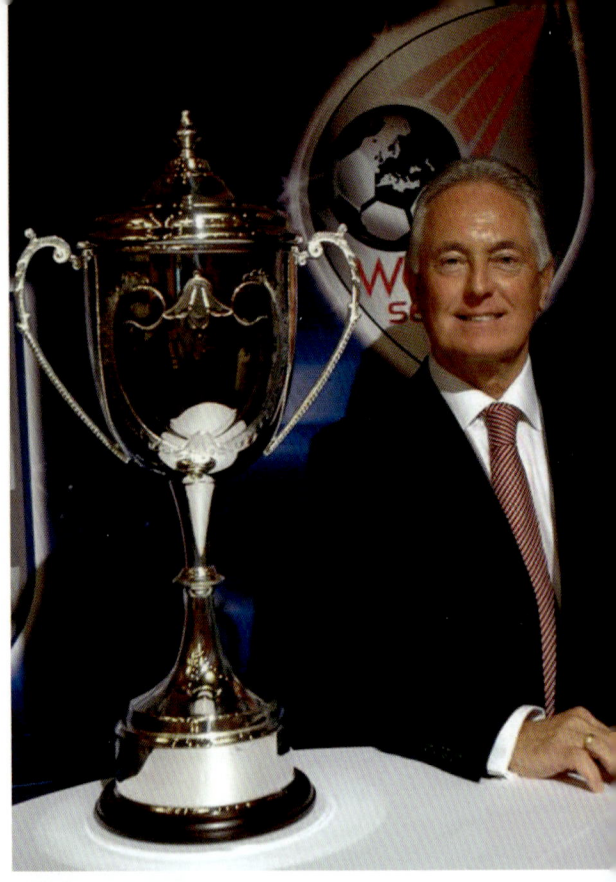

*Enjoying the good life …
at home in Marbella.*

10

A Strange Appointment

DAVE MACKAY was to pay a ludicrously high price for seeing Roger Davies, Franny Lee and Alan Hinton all depart over the summer of 1976. After promising so much going into the last few weeks of the season, with a potential League and FA Cup Double up for grabs, the 1975-76 campaign had ended in anticlimax. A home match against Stoke City one evening in March proved particularly cruel. The dropped point from a 1-1 draw was bad enough, but much worse was the dislocated shoulder that ruled out Charlie George, such a potent influence, for the remainder of the season. There followed the 2-0 FA Cup semi-final defeat by Tommy Docherty's young Manchester United side at Hillsborough before the season ended with Derby in fourth place, although Franny typically signed off with a flourish and two goals in a 6-2 win at Ipswich.

With cash to reinvest from the Davies deal, and wages freed up by the other two forwards leaving, Dave was at liberty to enter the transfer market again for another top striker to add to the quality of Charlie and Kevin Hector. The manager, though, placed a lot of faith in Jeff Bourne, who had caught his eye with goals galore on loan at Dallas Tornado. Jeff came back from action in the North American Soccer League with a suntan that was the envy of everyone in the dressing room, only to pull a hamstring in his first appearance.

Charlie George was back from injury but appeared ill at ease, getting himself sent off on the opening day of the season at Newcastle United, and collecting a club fine for his trouble. October arrived, Colin Todd asked for a transfer and had to be mollified by the promise of a long-term contract to give him the security he wanted. Misfortune mounted for Mackay when in a 1-0 defeat at Stoke, David Nish, our highly skilled left-back, suffered a knee injury that was to end his season.

Goals were in short supply and there was unrest in the dressing room at half-time at Birmingham City, where the team went down 5-1. Derby's opening eight League matches brought five draws and three defeats, disappointing but hardly disastrous, particularly as the side started to find their feet in front of goal, demolishing Finn Harps 12-0 in the UEFA Cup before Bruce Rioch, pushed into service as an emergency centre-forward, scored four times in an 8-2 victory over Tottenham. November came and the board was none too happy to find a lucrative source of revenue cut off when Derby went down in both legs of the UEFA Cup-tie with AEK Athens. The Greeks' 3-2 win in the second leg was Derby's first home defeat in Europe.

A STRANGE APPOINTMENT

I was even more disturbed to arrive at work to have a copy of *The Sun* shoved in front of my nose and read a short piece headlined "Beware of the Bogeyman" in which John Sadler revealed a contact had been playing golf with directors of an East Midlands club and that their manager could expect the sack any day now.

Dave saw the article, too, and stormed into a board meeting carrying the paper, pointing an accusing finger round the table and shouting: "You lot, you can stick your job up your arses," before making a hasty exit. The embarrassed silence was broken a few minutes later when Dave, having remembered that his claim to compensation would be tenuous if he resigned, returned to announce: "I won't resign. Screw the lot of you but you'll have to sack me." And sack Dave Mackay they did – ridiculously in my opinion – a little more than 18 months after cruising to the First Division title. On 25 November 1976, Dave and his assistant, Des Anderson, were shown the door. Dave told me: "Some of those directors are deluded. They've been spoilt rotten. They seriously expect a trophy every season now."

He was right, too. A football man who liked his players to be men, and treated them as such, Dave fell victim to some dirty work behind the scenes.

There was a lot of talk at Kedleston Golf Club, a home from home for some of the directors, about Dave drinking too much. I made it plain to vice-chairman George Hardy, the emerging power in the boardroom, that I felt Dave was an old-school genius from the class that worked hard and played hard. "What's the panic?" I wanted to know. "Only a few months ago we finished in the top four, reached the FA Cup semis and came within a goal of giving Real Madrid a nervous breakdown – and you're not happy with Dave?"

So what if the gaffer loved a drop of Mateus Rosé? It never detracted from his performance as a manager. Dave having an extra glass of wine on a Friday night was never going to stop Archie Gemmill running his bollocks off the following afternoon. We were a successful club with a good squad, and a reserve team holding their own near the top of the powerful Central League against the big guns in the North – Manchester United, Liverpool, Everton and Leeds. Actually, that was where his replacement was found.

With Dave Mackay sacked, Derby County urgently needed an experienced manager, but the board didn't look far. In fact, there didn't appear to be any real discussion about it. The decision seemed to have been made almost before Dave and Des had time to clear their desks. The directors turned to the Reserves' coach, Colin Murphy. Dario Gradi, a former amateur player and regional FA coach, was to be his assistant. It seemed a very strange appointment. Here we were, recent champions of England, into Europe, with a team of top-class players – some of them international stars – all strong characters who needed strong management, strong leadership, and there we were giving the job to the second team's coach. I thought the lesson had been learned when Manchester United appointed Wilf McGuinness to step into Sir Matt Busby's shoes.

That didn't end well, and, as I feared, things began to unravel at Derby County too. After Bruce Rioch, an inspired Mackay signing, left for Everton for £200,000, Derby spent £330,000 to sign centre-forward Derek Hales. Hales had an enviable

A STRANGE APPOINTMENT

goalscoring record at Charlton Athletic, a bit lower down football's food chain, but there he was regularly fed by a couple of wingers. In marked contrast, Derby's attacking approach had been based around possession, and passes threaded through for first John O'Hare and later Franny Lee to control and bring others around them into play.

Like Leighton James before him, Hales was not a good fit. In fact he was a costly mistake. It was indicative of the inexperience in the boardroom and in the manager's office. I felt that the answer to Derby's immediate problems resided on Merseyside in a modest 1930s semi-detached house in Bellefield Avenue in the West Derby suburb of Liverpool ... the home of Bill Shankly.

* * * * *

Dressed in his grey suit and red tie, Bill paced the Derby County dressing room on a matchday in the winter of 1976-77, his face wreathed in a smile, hands thrust deep into his trouser pockets.

Every so often, he stooped to growl: "I want you cutting the front lawn tomorrow, son," and a white-shirted player nodded obediently.

His pre-match work over, Shanks disappeared, leaving a bemused team asking each other: "Cutting the front lawn? What on earth is he on about?" They thought that the great manager was talking gibberish.

You see, Bill was familiar and comfortable with an era when players came from the local town, they all drank in the local pub, their wives went about their business in the local shops, and after a good win, those players could get the lawnmower out of the shed on a Sunday afternoon, stick out their chests and give the front lawn a trim, safe in the knowledge of favourable comments from every passer-by.

Shanks rebuked me as a "terrier" and a "pain in the arse" as I badgered him into coming down from Merseyside to help out. I knew that the Liverpool legend was delighted at being wanted – but Colin Murphy did not appreciate the move. It was the loose appointment of an elder statesman whose vast knowledge and experience could be tapped into. But I think that Murphy felt threatened.

Why, I don't know. After all, Shanks was pushing 65. He didn't want all the hassle of going back anywhere near the coalface of the First Division. He just wanted to keep an involvement in football and be part of a successful team. In turn, Derby County could have done with his help.

Unfortunately, having successfully engineered an advisory role for Shanks at the Baseball Ground, I didn't get the necessary support for what I was trying to achieve. There were a few knockers about, whispering: "What's he bringing Bill in for?" It wasn't accepted for what it was – that the great Shanks would be with us for six months or so. It wasn't forever.

Over the years, when he ruled Anfield, Bill had taken to me. Josie and I used to wait while having breakfast on a Sunday morning for the phone to ring at 11am. She always answered and exchanged pleasantries before handing over the receiver, whispering: "Your Scottish pal is on the phone."

Shanks would say: "How yer doin', son. Aye, I see you drew yesterday. You're having a tough time at the moment, aren't you, son? You need somebody playing deeper in midfield. That Hector's a good player. We must talk, aye."

A STRANGE APPOINTMENT

Bill loved all the Derby players, especially his fellow Scot, Archie Gemmill, and Kevin Hector, so it was natural that I would think of him when I was looking for someone to give Murphy and Gradi a bit of help. He had been so disappointed in the manner of his departure at Anfield. I saw an opportunity that he wanted another platform and his age allowed him to do it.

I worked on Bill for weeks and weeks to persuade him to come, suggesting how good it would be for him to be back in the game.

You're not going to pick the phone up and it happens overnight. Shanks was a football god, a super manager, and I would have walked to Derby with him on my back if needs be.

"Come and be part of the team for six months here, Bill," I told him. "Get yourself out of Liverpool. Come to Derby, jazz it up a bit."

Eventually, Shanks simply could not resist the challenge and agreed to a part-time consultancy on Fridays and Saturdays. On 16 December, the morning after a sterile goalless home draw against Arsenal, the *Daily Mirror* broke the news: "Derby send for Shanks."

We paid for a chauffeur, his mate, to do the driving, while Bill was happy to accept peanuts in place of a proper salary. He didn't want much more than the cost of his meals and overnight accommodation covering. "Aye, Stuart, the money's not important," he told me over a pre-match lunch with the players. "I'm in football for the great glory, son."

In truth, he did very little at Derby because he wasn't encouraged by Murphy and Gradi to be part of it. It was a shame. They didn't embrace him and unless people embraced the plan, he and I were wasting our time. The relationship drifted away.

The new year of 1977 began with Colin Murphy confirmed as Derby County's manager, George Hardy now satisfied that he had done enough to merit the caretaker prefix to his job description being dropped. Six weeks later, however, the chairman changed his mind, having witnessed Derek Hales splutter into life with two goals in a win over Newcastle but the team struggle to eliminate Blackpool and Colchester in FA Cup replays and at one stage stumble to 19th in the table following defeats by Middlesbrough, Manchester United, Leeds and Liverpool.

The scene was set for a dramatic return. Or at least the promise of one ...

11

Cloughie's Big Stitch Up

IN 1977, the late actor Peter Finch was awarded a posthumous Oscar for his role in *Network*, but I doubt that he had put on a better performance than Brian Clough did at the Baseball Ground on Tuesday, 22 February that year.

"I've decided I'm not coming," he told the Derby County directors. "I've just painted Nigel's rabbit hutch red, so how can I leave our Nigel's rabbits with a red hutch and come back to Derby and play in white? How can I let our Nigel and Simon down?"

Vice-chairman George Hardy was crestfallen as Clough, pretending to look equally disappointed, left to explain his decision to stay at Nottingham Forest. Barrie Eccleston, from BBC Radio Derby, asked: "Was there ever a time you felt you might join Derby today?"

Clough said: "There was never a time when I didn't feel that, apart from right at the end. I wanted to come back to Derby so badly it was unbelievable." I don't know how he kept a straight face.

It was all an act, of course – a carefully rehearsed act for the fans, and for the media.

Mind you, the Derby board got what they deserved for the shabby manner in which they had engineered Dave Mackay's departure and then followed it with the surprising appointment of Colin Murphy as his successor. Hardy made a big play of bringing Brian Clough back to the Baseball Ground. Reinstating Cloughie as manager would have been a tremendous coup for the millionaire scrap metal merchant who loved to bowl around in a Rolls-Royce bearing personalised number plates. His stock with the fans would have gone through the roof. But he turned out not to be a knight in shining armour, mounted on a white charger, riding to the rescue after all.

Despite being sickened by the manner of Mackay's demise, I have always known you have to be practical in football. There are no prizes for sentiment and I thought that trying for Brian was a good move, providing he wasn't using us for other things. My worst fears were realised. He *was* using us, of course, whether to settle old scores or improve his financial situation at the City Ground. It was probably a bit of both.

I am certain that Brian's conditions for what Rams supporters would have regarded as a Second Coming were harsh. He wanted Sam Longson kicked off the board and me out of the club. Hardy and his directors were so keen to get him that I might well have left. But it never came to that.

Looking back, for Brian Clough to say that he always wanted to walk back through the doors of the Baseball Ground to stay was, frankly, incredible. After he read the *Daily Mirror's* back page headline: "Derby plea to ex-boss... Cloughie come home!" how he must have relished the sort of power enjoyed by Roman emperors who made life-changing decisions by thumb. As Roy McFarland, club skipper at the time, astutely observed: "George Hardy was led up the garden path."

Hardy had to eat more humble pie by telling Murphy and Dario Gradi that their jobs were safe, although Sam Longson, who immediately resigned as chairman to become president, insisted that his successor, Hardy, and the board were still determined to reinstate the Clough-Peter Taylor partnership. Meanwhile, Murphy laboured on, and we looked weak, on and off the pitch. Rival clubs sensed that there might be some easy pickings, Stoke City chancing their arm with an unsuccessful bid for Charlie George.

Knowing that Hardy was now in no position to resist his rebuilding plans, Murphy went shopping to Manchester and bagged Gerry Daly for £175,000. The Irish international was delighted to escape Old Trafford after a serious falling-out with manager Tommy Docherty. If only the midfielder had access to a crystal ball, he might have run a mile in a different direction.

* * * * *

Easter 1977 was a hugely rewarding personal time for me as Derby County were able to announce the £300,000 sponsorship deal I had concluded with Saab, although we failed to get approval to use the name of the Swedish car manufacturers on our shirts the following season. The FA refused to allow shirt advertising because of their commitments to the TV companies, and Arsenal chairman Denis Hill-Wood in particular, an influential voice at Lancaster Gate, objected on the grounds that it would "prostitute the League and the club, and those wonderful shirts of the time". Hill-Wood's son, Peter, succeeded him as chairman in 1982, when Denis passed away, and held the post until June 2013 ... seven years after Arsenal moved into the Emirates Stadium. What was that about prostitution? Where we led, others followed, and, once we had set the bandwagon rolling, Arsenal were one of the first to jump aboard.

I'd seen the positive effect that shirt sponsorship could have on clubs' finances abroad, particularly in Italy where Gianni Agnelli had the name of Fiat emblazoned across those famous black-and-white shirts of Juventus. It was happening in Europe, but not in England, and so I decided to try to drive it forward on these shores. In eight years we had been Football League champions (twice in four seasons) and had finished in the top four on three other occasions, and that meant I was able to speak at the top table. I talked to Hitachi, Texaco, Saab and Walt Disney. In the end we went with Saab because they were offering us the most money, perhaps just as well because we'd have looked a bit daft with Mickey Mouse plastered across our shirts.

Part of the Saab deal stipulated that we'd be given 22 cars a year and, with several big-name stars' contracts up for negotiation around that time, I spotted an opportunity to save the club some money. The implicit instruction from the boardroom and myself to Murphy was that the club was going to be hard on these players and that they were to be offered a top-of-the-range Saab rather than a top-up in salary. They were already well paid and several had underperformed in what had been a dismal campaign. One by one, they all trooped in to see Colin … and one by one they left his office buoyed by a pay rise *and* a Saab. The bargaining tool of the car was meant to save the club thousands of pounds but instead it was completely wasted. But that was how things worked back then with the manager handling contracts.

I look back on the deal with Saab as perhaps my most important contribution to English football. I mean, look where sponsorship within the game is today. Just about every club has a main kit sponsor, and some have different home and away backers. No one could have dared forecast in their wildest dreams that one day Manchester United would agree a mammoth £750million kit manufacturing and sponsorship arrangement with adidas to run for a decade from the 2015-16 season.

As a club we were extremely happy with the deal, and so were our sponsors who put everything behind it in terms of public relations. At the launch we had a number of glamorous models draped over our players and cars on the Baseball Ground pitch, and on Fridays before away fixtures we'd often visit showrooms and garages in whichever city we were in. It was the start of sponsorship as we know it today and Derby County, again, were there at the beginning.

In the second year of the deal I was right up against it with Saab because the contract stated that the cars were for the players, yet one or two had given them to their wives. On the whole, though, it was hugely positive for both parties and, on a personal level, extremely satisfying and very exciting. It was my contribution to the club, to the team effort, and I always felt it was as important as the manager winning the FA Charity Shield, as it was known then, or a player scoring a big goal.

For some time Liverpool had also been looking into the possibility of shirt sponsorship, and after we'd agreed our deal with Saab my friend Peter Robinson, their chief executive and one of the most respected officials in football, moved quickly, striking one of his own with Hitachi. Arsenal, having objected so vociferously, soon had their own deal too.

While shirt sponsorship was my domain, kit manufacturing deals were not, although I was instrumental in introducing a new logo of a vibrant ram. I'd be kept abreast of what was being agreed, and with whom, but in those days it was down to the manager to sort it out as part of the technical side of the game. If I wanted a particular strip I could certainly have my say, but if the manager said: "No, it's too thick, it won't be comfortable for my players," then I'd have to go with his decision. Patrick, Admiral, Le Coq Sportif – those were the sort of firms we'd be dealing with. Managers would sort it out, and they probably got a little deal out of it, a kick-back in a plastic bag as a thank you from grateful manufacturers. We got peanuts for kit deals in those days, though; nothing like the multi-million pound agreements struck now.

But money was now coming into the game, and secretaries and chief executives looked at football with a commercial eye rather than simply saying: "Me? I just do what I'm told, file the paperwork." People like myself, Peter Robinson at Liverpool, and Eddie Plumley, who went on to work at Watford with Elton John, could see the reach that football had. We wanted to push the boundaries of the game and explore the emerging commercial opportunities.

✻ ✻ ✻ ✻ ✻ ✻

CLOUGHIE'S BIG STITCH UP

Sadly, at Derby, success off the field was not being matched on it, and only seven months after the shenanigans with Clough, the club decided the time was right for a managerial change. I've never believed that Colin Murphy should have been given the job, but I also know that the structure of the club at the time – something that the board should have addressed – was also part of the problem. There's no question that Murphy was a good coach, an FA coach. Under a very good, strong manager he and Gradi running another part of the club would undoubtedly have worked.

Let's say Dave Mackay had stayed in charge of the first team with Colin running the reserves and Dario the academy: we'd have had a wonderful set-up. Unfortunately no one had the foresight to make that a reality. Over the years Dario has proved his brilliance in developing young talent: David Platt, Rob Jones and Geoff Thomas all enjoyed a thorough grounding under him at Crewe Alexandra and went on to play for England.

There have been many more who had great careers at the top of the domestic game after learning their trade from him. Imagine if he'd had five or ten years nurturing the best young talent in and beyond Derbyshire, feeding them on to Colin in the reserves and he in turn, when they were ready, on to Dave at the top. But there were no youth academies back then, the kids had no real chance to develop.

There were youth teams, of course, but neither time nor effort was put into them. Managers just bought players for the first team, clubs wanted instant success. I hear the criticism aimed at clubs now because of their apparent failure to bring through young players, particularly young English players, but at least they are having a go; at least there are now academy programmes in place to try to make it happen.

Back then, by and large, it was ignored. It was a case of buy a player, slot him in, last piece of the jigsaw and all that. The manager was scouting for the first team only. There wasn't any planning.

Colin's main problem was that there was always a feeling that he wasn't going to be there long, and even though you could see him working hard to get the players' respect, you knew it wasn't going to happen for him.

Off the field it had become a time of change for me as well, despite our commercial success. With George Hardy now chairman I felt as though I was having to prove myself all over again. My job became difficult because the machinery wasn't now running smoothly. Where Sam Longson placed a lot of trust in me and allowed me to do deals and work on my own for the good of the club, I had to refer far too much to George. With all due respect to him, he had to refer to the board, because he was the new chairman, the new boy on the block. He wasn't experienced at executive level in football. He was learning the ropes, and so he had to answer to his board on many run-of-the-mill issues.

Sam had his faults, yet his instincts and gut reaction were frequently spot on. He was a very good businessman and he allowed Brian Clough and his other managers to get on with things. He was very supportive and he controlled the board of directors very well. He was one of them, but he knew what he wanted. Yes, Brian finally drove him to distraction, but in the early days when Brian was out and about on the prowl for a player, Sam would say: "Let's not piss about now, Stuart. Let's get it done. Let's beat Liverpool, let's beat Man United."

Some of Derby's most notable transfers has materialised as if out of thin air, thanks to the brilliance of managers like Brian Clough and Dave Mackay. Now a fog had descended over affairs at the Baseball Ground, and a catastrophic managerial change wasn't about to make matters any clearer.

12

Doc's Quick Fix

ONLY TWO points from their first five matches – one of them a crushing 3-0 defeat at the hands of newly promoted Nottingham Forest – left Derby County looking for a football miracle worker in 1977-78. Brian Clough and Peter Taylor were shifting the balance of power in the East Midlands, but George Hardy now knew that they were beyond his reach.

For all his shortcomings, Colin Murphy should have been taken to one side, told things weren't working and gently dismissed. Instead, he was in the Baseball Ground dugout, biting his nails as we hung on for a 2-2 draw with Leeds United while Tommy Docherty, his successor, was being entertained over drinks and cigars in the boardroom. It wasn't professional or pleasant, but when the change was put to me as a done deal, I was by no means against the idea of the Doc coming in as a short-term fix. Derby County had gone flat and I thought here was a man who had the cheek, the chatter and the bounce to reverse a downward trend. I had heard enough managers elsewhere demand: "I need a five-year contract because this job will take that long to turn it around, Mr Chairman, and I'm your man." Tommy wasn't like that. Five years was a life sentence to him. From day one he knew the score at Derby, and because of what he was and who he was, I thought that he could succeed for maybe a year, possibly two. Certainly time enough for us to get a long-term strategy in place and think in terms of challenging for the title again.

What happened was little short of a disaster. I thought he might shake things up, bring in a couple of stars. It didn't work and there were so many comings and goings, the Baseball Ground needed a revolving door fitted.

The Doc had been out of the spotlight since Manchester United sacked him for his affair with Mary Brown, the Old Trafford physiotherapist's wife – who he later married. At Derby he changed the playing staff too quickly. Too many stars disappeared and the transition was brutal. Tommy was a laugh but he wouldn't listen to anybody. Not a lot of thought went into what he was doing. He just wanted changes: old players out, new players in. In only 12 months he completed no less than 30 transfer deals – 14 in and 16 out, the 16th provoking a great deal of sadness among supporters who saw the incomparable Colin Todd sold to Everton for £330,000.

When Docherty had finished his root and branch clearance, there was no Todd, no Archie Gemmill, no Charlie George, no Kevin Hector, no Colin Boulton and no Leighton James. James was Derby's first £300,000 player but he went to QPR in exchange for Don Masson who, a year later, was allowed to move to Notts County on a free transfer. The club lost a fortune on Derek Hales, the £330,000 misfit who was sold to West Ham United for £110,000. It was madness, financial suicide. No way to run a business.

Against the odds, the Doc struck a truce with an old sparring partner, Gerry Daly. In the early days, Tommy referred to his midfield trio of Daly, Masson and Bruce Rioch as "my three Van Goghs" but the writing was on the wall. At a club of Derby's size, with a limited budget, you can't make too many mistakes before the knives are out. Dave Mackay discovered that when he placed an undue amount of faith in Jeff Bourne.

Gung-ho Docherty rattled along at a ridiculous pace, shooting from the lip with a crack a minute. When he put his head round the dressing-room door and said: "Hello, whoever you are," it might have brought a laugh from guys such as Vic Moreland and Billy Caskey, from Glentoran, two of the weird and wonderful signings the manager convinced the board were going to change the world, but it brought little more than a painful wince from a man such as loyal club captain Roy McFarland.

At the press conference to introduce him, Tommy was quizzed about his worst day in football. He once tried to sue Willie Morgan, the case collapsed and he had to admit to lying. "When I was in the High Court, coming down the lift on the third day of the trial, the guy in the lift said: 'Are you going down, sir?' I said: 'I hope not.'"

One reporter wanted to know: "What's it like to follow Colin Murphy and Dario Gradi?"

"I thought they were a ceilidh band."

It brought the house down.

DOC'S QUICK FIX

Please understand that Tom wasn't the spiv that some people liked to paint him, but Derby's plight was deadly serious with trouble on the pitch and off it. Money problems dictated that we could not afford to ignore any offer, and we readily accepted a trip to Baghdad to tackle the Iraq national team in a friendly. Not something an English club will replicate any time soon, sadly. Greece and Egypt were other countries to give Derby County a warm welcome – we were often in demand – and the oil-rich Middle East was particularly attractive, another revenue stream, given the sums mentioned to travel out to the desert. As I told Gerald Mortimer in the *Derby Evening Telegraph* in November 1977: "There is plenty of money available in that part of the world. They are trying to develop their football and are extremely keen for top English sides to go over and play."

We mulled over invitations to Qatar and Kuwait the following month, the Qatari offer a result of the fact that former Derby forward Frank Wignall was in charge of the national team. Frank and his employers wanted both our first team and juniors to face their national team and an age-group national team on the same evening. I was sorry to have to knock back Frank, not something many bruised and battered defenders managed in his prime, but Kuwait were gazumped by a superior offer from the Iraqi FA.

Around 45,000 Iraqis packed the national stadium to watch us but the game was a damp squib, ending 0-0. Far more eventful was the return journey because Frank Blunstone, Doc's assistant, lost his passport and had a nervous ordeal explaining to Iraq's military police why he was trying to get back to Britain without the necessary documentation. And, more importantly, what he was doing in their country without a passport. Poor old Frank spent ten hours trying to negotiate his way out of a fraught situation before British Embassy officials successfully intervened.

* * * * *

Whenever a manager is hyperactive in the transfer market, there are accusations of money going missing, and the Doc wasn't immune to the whispers. With problems mounting, factions developed at all levels of the club, nowhere more so than in the boardroom. They came to a head when Tommy took the players on an end-of-season tour to Mallorca. I went out halfway through the trip to pay some bills, and ensure that everything was running smoothly. While I was out of the country, one of the Derby directors brought in the police to investigate what they believed to be some dodgy transfer deals. Tom was buying and selling at a rare old pace, a couple of players had gone to America, and the Derbyshire Constabulary was looking for evidence of corruption.

I took a telephone call in Spain to inform me of developments and when I got back to England I went to see the police to ask what was going on. They wanted me to help with their enquiries. "Well, there's my office," I told them. "Feel free to get on with it. Just tell me when you need me." I was told I'd be better off at home that week. As I had absolutely nothing to hide, I replied: "You know the address. Give me a call if you need me."

It was a contrived situation, and I thought: "What's going on here? What am I doing? This is crazy." I told Sam Longson that, in my opinion, this was all part of the same plan, going right back to when other directors had tried to unnerve him and forced him to resign as chairman. He agreed that there was an undercurrent of malign forces. I took a deep breath and told Sam: "Do you know what? I don't need this." I resigned and stepped down. It was a classic case of the board squabbling, I was the chief executive but I felt that I could no longer work with these people. Josie and I had just started Lonsdale and I decided that I would throw myself into our travel business. We had persuaded John Cheadle to join us from Co-op Travel in Derby and we began to create what was to become a highly successful travel group. I wanted to concentrate on what I do well and forget about the football club's pathetic politics. It was a horrific time for Derby County.

Then one day, out of the blue, Chief Superintendent Jim Reddington, who was heading the probe and who I had got to know quite well, came to me and said: "Look Stuart, we've conducted a vigorous 18-month investigation into the affairs of the club. We've visited the US. We've interviewed numerous managers and directors from other clubs, and we're satisfied with our findings. We've found nothing improper at all. We're going to make a statement confirming that we are closing the case and that there has been no wrongdoing at Derby County FC."

I knew all along there was nothing to find, but still the relief was palpable. "Well, it has wasted 18 months of my life but thank goodness it's all OK," I told him. Had I stayed at the club, waiting for the endgame, I would have wasted even more of my time. Now at least I was free to focus with greater intensity on Lonsdale, where things were really taking off. Twenty or so years later, I received letters from a couple of the board members who had been involved. They apologised for the part they had played and their actions during that shoddy period. These were serious businessmen but they got caught up in the football bubble and were worse directors for it.

Qualified accountant Richard Moore, whose family owned the Coxmoore Knitwear firm, was a decent guy but he was part of the group fighting Sam. He accepted that he should probably have taken more of a stand, telling his colleagues: "Hey, come on, this is a well-run club, let's get this sorted internally." But, instead, he was swayed by misguided emotions. He wrote to me, saying: "Look, your life has turned out fantastically, but one or two of us didn't stand up at the time when probably we should have. But you made the right decision getting out." It was a nice letter, a nice touch.

As for Tommy, I never got the impression that he cared much about Derby County. The club wasn't in his blood. And he was at the end of his career – a very successful career one has to say – and he had married Mary. He was besotted with her. They'd moved to Derbyshire and he couldn't wait to get away from the ground in the afternoon to be with her. On his way home, he frequently called at Bob Chambers, an Ashbourne florist, to collect a magnificent bunch of flowers for his new wife. He viewed Derby as a winding-down position, a retirement plan, while we were crying out for a man with the opposite set of values.

The Doc left in May 1979, after 20 months at the club, with Derby County in 19th position, one place above the relegated trio of Chelsea, Birmingham and QPR. The rot had set in. Derby went down the following season under Colin Addison. His assistant, John Newman, took over at a club where there was precious little money to spend and where public interest was at a low ebb compared to the heady days of just a few years earlier. As early as the November of 1982, Derby found themselves facing a struggle to stay in the Second Division. Then the new chairman, Mike Watterson – who had made a name for himself as a snooker impresario – brought back a couple of familiar faces. Mike asked me if I would consider a return to the club as a director and chief executive, and after a year away I couldn't resist the temptation to take up his offer.

He was complimentary about what I had to offer and paid me this nice tribute in *The Ram*:

> *We have brought back yet another architect of the Rams' former success – Stuart Webb. Acknowledged to be among the very few top administrators in the game, he will be a tower of strength in the boardroom, where harmony and unity of purpose now reigns. And that is another vital asset. Stuart is too, a top marketing and promotions expert. This club needs his talent and his personality in this most vital of sectors. Fundraising in this day and age is the life-blood of any League club, however big. We are delighted to have 'recaptured' him.*

Between us, Mike and I then convinced Peter Taylor to put his retirement on hold and come back to Derby as manager. Peter's first foray into football management had come at Burton Albion, where he spent three years before teaming up with his old playing partner Brian Clough at Hartlepool, following him to Derby, then Brighton and Forest. He was a massive influence on Brian. They were a double act, unbeatable together in their prime. Without

Peter, Brian was half the man. Peter was the steadying influence in the relationship, and Brian leant on Peter more than Peter needed Brian. With Peter by his side, Old Big 'Ed would certainly have lasted a lot longer than 44 days at Leeds United.

Peter could never have been the manager Brian was but, without Peter, Brian really was only half the manager. The former goalkeeper was good at analysing players, both as footballers and as characters. The players loved his sense of humour on and off the training field. When things became rocky between Brian and myself, he was the go-between and I had a lot to do with Peter. He realised the three of us needed to work together. If Peter had gone with him to Elland Road, Brian might have prospered because I'm certain that Pete, with his gruff charm and humour, could have won over that dressing room of Billy Bremner, Johnny Giles and Co. Instead he chose to stay down on the south coast at the Goldstone Ground, stepping up to the manager's job when Brian headed to Yorkshire.

Taylor and Clough were reunited in July 1976 when, having led Brighton to fourth in the old Third Division, Peter left to team up with his old mate at Nottingham Forest. The partners made history there, the sort we hoped they were going to make at Derby before things turned so sour. Under their guidance, Forest were promoted to the First Division, became champions of England and went on to win the European Cup twice, an incredible achievement, before Peter retired in May 1982.

Now, knowing him as I did, I had the inside track on Peter. He would be a little lost without football and when I made contact with him I wasn't wrong. Even so, he still took some persuading that he was the man for the job at Derby County. A year earlier,

DOC'S QUICK FIX

he and Brian had parted company on good terms at the City Ground. Naturally, they had been through more than their fair share of ups and downs, and at one stage the £1million failure of Justin Fashanu at Forest pushed their relationship to the limit. But, by and large, things were OK between them.

Soon after Peter arrived at Derby, however, a wedge was driven between them that became a chasm. Peter was clear from the off that we needed a big-name signing, and wanted to bring in a player to give the dressing room a lift, a jolt. In June 1983, he identified John Robertson as that man. Robertson had joined Forest in 1970 and at 30 was getting on a bit, but Peter felt he still possessed a touch of magic. So he made his move to bring a player once described by Clough as "an artist, a Picasso" to the Baseball Ground. What upset Clough so much was the fact that Taylor didn't bother to inform him. And, without a doubt, Peter knew how much of a problem it would cause. We all did. But Peter wanted Robertson. He thought that he'd do well for Derby … and to hell with the consequences. That's why Peter pounced while Cloughie was away on a 100-mile charity walk through the Yorkshire Dales that summer.

Don't get me wrong. It wasn't done to spite Brian. We just wanted what was best for Derby County. It was like when we signed Charlie George from under Tottenham's noses. We didn't do it to upset Spurs. We did it because we thought it would benefit Derby.

So if it upset Brian, it upset him. Pete had spoken to John – he'd tapped him. You don't go for somebody unless you do the groundwork and certainly not in this sort of situation, given the ructions it would inevitably cause. Peter felt that John would come because he was winding down his contract at Forest and feared he would be offered reduced terms to stay there. John fancied the generous three-year deal on offer at Derby, so he gave Peter the nod to set it all up. Of course, we knew what to expect when Brian arrived at the pub he was staying at on the Saturday night, to be told in a telephone call to his wife Barbara what we had done. He was soon on the line to Peter, screaming, shouting. He went ballistic.

Rightly or wrongly, Cloughie felt betrayed by both Taylor and Robertson, but if he'd treated Robbo better and not kept him up in the air over a proposed two-year extension at Forest, I don't believe that the Scottish winger would have entertained the prospect of jumping ship and crossing the great divide.

"He's starting his antics. Put your tin hat on," Pete warned me. We had them at the ready, but I was relaxed about any reprisals because, in getting the star attraction Peter craved, we had not broken any rules. Sadly, no one emerged from the saga with their reputation enhanced. Because he was always "Forest" in the eyes of more than a few on the Derby terraces, I felt that Robbo was up against it from the word go. Peter's judgment, razor-sharp earlier as a talent-spotter supreme, was at fault because the player was just past his sell-by date.

Apart from his not inconsiderable wages, Robbo cost us £135,000 at a transfer tribunal in London – not a day I care to remember at the Great Western Hotel, Paddington, with any fondness. In fairness, a cartilage operation didn't help matters and he scored four goals, two of them penalties, in 83 appearances spread across two seasons before returning to Forest on a free transfer.

Before he was sacked, Peter was honest enough to tell me: "I'm sorry, Stuart, he's shot it."

The rift between Peter and Brian lasted considerably longer than John Robertson at Derby County, Clough branding Taylor a "a snake in the grass" in a newspaper interview, adding: "We pass each other on the A52 going to work most days of the week. But if his car broke down and I saw him thumbing a lift, I wouldn't pick him up, I'd run him over."

The pair still weren't on speaking terms when Peter died suddenly in his holiday flat in Mallorca, aged 62, in October 1990, from pulmonary fibrosis – a respiratory disease diagnosed three years earlier. Brian was inconsolable and deeply regretted not having made it up with his old pal. Like everyone, I have fallen out with people on occasion, but Brian's reaction to Peter's death reinforced in me something I sincerely believe in: look after those who are nearest and dearest to you. Life's too short.

13

Judgment Day

THE AUTUMN of 1983 found Derby County all at sea, not so much waving as drowning. By the end of October, following a 2-1 home defeat by Grimsby Town which attracted, if that is the right word, an attendance of 11,688, Peter Taylor's side had lost eight of their 12 matches in the Second Division.

Hopes of progress in the League Cup sank without trace in the form of a 7-0 aggregate thrashing by Birmingham City. The mood of the players was not helped by a delay in their wages being paid.

Mike Watterson had left, John Kirkland taking over as chairman. It was worse – much worse – than a case of the doldrums behind the scenes. Our board meetings were routinely held at the Baseball Ground, but on this occasion John summoned everybody to Heage, to the impressive headquarters of Bowmer & Kirkland, his construction business. John's company accountant also managed Derby County's company books and records.

JUDGMENT DAY

It was a lonely, uncomfortable drive out to the countryside and I felt extremely apprehensive because I wasn't at all sure what, exactly, was coming. What I did know was that it wouldn't be a sweet pill. I was uncomfortable because I prided myself on being able to read situations and gauge moods. As chief executive, I should have suspected something was amiss. I soon found out.

His hands shaking with emotion, Kirkland said: "I have to report that we are insolvent. The club is losing money on a weekly basis and we cannot continue. I have taken advice and the only way forward is to appoint a receiver." The door opened and in walked representatives of Peat, Marwick, Mitchell & Co, the accountants who had recently acted as official receiver of Wolverhampton Wanderers. They came straight to the point: "Gentlemen, in technical terms, you are trading illegally. On a monthly basis, you are spending more money than is coming in, and to continue would not be in the best interests of the shareholders."

I looked around the table at the other directors: Bill Hart, Fred Fern, Chris Charlton, successful local businessmen who had supported the club financially over the years. They looked shell-shocked. Trevor East, Derby-born and bred, a lifelong fan and senior executive at Sky Sports, looked dejected. Trevor had been extremely supportive to me over the years, particularly during my time as managing director, and had vast contacts within the game. He seemed to sense that the position was insurmountable.

I had recently introduced Geoff Glossop to the club as a potential director. I knew Geoff through his software company in which I had an interest. Incredibly, this was his first board meeting. He had committed funds, around £200,000. "Hell," I thought, "it's all going pear-shaped even before Geoff has been confirmed as a director."

Kirkland said: "In the circumstances, I feel I have no option but to stand down." John and his family had a long relationship with the club. His decision had not been taken lightly. Total silence. It was one of those watershed moments. I wasn't having it. We may have resembled a sinking ship but the last thing we needed was deserters. "No resignations," I insisted. "You have to continue as chairman, John. The board must stay together to demonstrate solidarity. Otherwise, the club won't survive." The other directors glumly nodded. I felt my head beginning to throb with the gravity of Derby County's plight.

Given some of the transfer fees and wages paid out by Peter Taylor for players, and the declining attendances that were due to the scourge of hooliganism that dogged football in general, it didn't need a genius to figure out that we were losing money. In fact, we were haemorrhaging the stuff.

Debts owed to the Inland Revenue, the Customs and Excise authority – who were chasing us over unpaid VAT – and other creditors amounted to more than £500,000, while a further £750,000 was due to NatWest Bank.

It was a frightening position. In boxing terms we weren't just on the ropes, we were at nine of the referee's count of ten. I shook my head, trying to focus, and I continued to make my case that I thought the club could still be salvaged. To my delight, Geoff spoke up and said the same. He stated that he'd honour his commitment to join the board and invest as promised. What a star. That gave me the lifeline we needed and the atmosphere around the table changed immediately as the directors, one by

JUDGMENT DAY

one, realised that chucking in the towel was not an option. I asked the accountants for a realistic timetable in which I could mount or deliver a rescue package, and stated that it was my intention that the board of directors should stay together and show solidarity during this process. To his credit John Kirkland, the chairman, along with the other directors, agreed to my plan of action.

I forced open a six-week window with the accountants to launch the lifeboats, and my first port of call was Nottingham, a short drive to see Football League president Jack Dunnett, a former Labour MP and also the president of Notts County. Looking back, I was quite brutal, as I told him: "Look, we're in the shit. You're going to lose a club here, mate, have a corpse on your hands, one of your founder members. Pull your finger out."

Dunnett's digit worked wonders, pointing me in the direction of London – and Robert Maxwell. He already owned Oxford United, and speculation was rife that he was stalking bigger prey in the form of Manchester United and Leeds United. Maxwell's secretary might have been the admin world's answer to Norman Hunter, so effective was she in blunting my every attempt to get through to the business magnate.

Then a Christmas card arrived at my Lonsdale travel agency, addressed to me personally, signed: "Bob, Elizabeth and family," and handwritten by Maxwell himself. That secretary sounded noticeably warmer when, days later, she phoned to arrange an evening meeting with Maxwell in his offices in the heart of the City of London. I left Josie and Beverley during the interval of *Singin' In The Rain,* starring Tommy Steele at the London Palladium, hailed a taxi to Worship Street, to be greeted by a security man and a Filipina housemaid, who escorted me in the lift to luxurious, top-floor accommodation.

Maxwell loomed from the far corner of a huge lobby and summoned me into his private dining room. I thought he might impress me with a nice bottle of fine wine but he wasn't much of a drinker, even though he liked to give the impression he was. He drank coffee from a pint pot with 'The Boss' inscribed on it. He sat at the head of the table, me to his right. A waitress tiptoed in with a menu of three choices, not much. I plumped for chicken salad and it arrived swiftly with Maxwell's choice, which he scoffed at an alarming rate. He was far removed from the image of a refined diner. "Fire away," he said, forcing me to abandon the remainder of my meal, although I did get a glass of white wine to oil the wheels as I explained my plans to save Derby County from extinction, and specifically why I felt he could help.

Social tittle-tattle was out of the question, he was switched on, totally focused, and he told me: "How very discouraging to find such a famous club on its knees and heading for the knacker's yard. I'll do what I can and get back to you."

Then he surprised me by leaning forward, seeking close eye contact, to enquire: "How old will you be at the turn of the century, Stuart? I will be an old man then." I told him that I was 42 and he wanted to know, as a matter of urgency: "Will you and I ever fall out?"

"I can't answer that," I told him, and he shook his head slowly, looking at his watch as he ushered me towards the lift before taking my private telephone numbers and promising to stay in touch. My 60-minute time slot had expired and, although it was well into the evening when I left, the Maxwell empire was still a

JUDGMENT DAY

hive of activity with secretaries working, phones ringing and fax machines churning. I was astonished to find myself back out on a wet, damp Worship Street in under an hour.

I had arranged to meet my wife and daughter later in Joe Allen, the famous Covent Garden haunt of theatregoers in search of a bite to eat. I'd warned Josie: "It could be a long one. I don't want you hanging around." So I booked a table and said: "If it's 11 o'clock, at least you're having your supper." But when they arrived around 10.15pm, I was already sitting there. Josie was concerned. "Did it not go well?" she enquired. "No … better than that," I replied, grinning from ear to ear, "it went fantastically well."

Negotiating with Maxwell was always a fraught affair. One day in Worship Street I was alarmed to discover Martin Edwards, the Manchester United chairman, walking out of one door as I was going in another. We were like those characters forecasting the weather: in for rain, out for sun, as we exchanged nervous half-smiles, much like patients at the dentist's surgery. That's how Maxwell loved to run his empire: keeping everyone on their toes, buying and selling three or four businesses a day if he could. Incredible …

By Christmas, Derby County's debt had risen to £1.5million, yet we stayed in regular contact and Maxwell was on the point of throwing his considerable financial weight behind the salvage operation in 1984 – the club's centenary year – when both the Inland Revenue and the VAT people issued writs against the club. They were chasing payments of £131,948 and £78,123 respectively. A winding-up petition meant our company bank accounts were frozen and any money received from this point had to be dealt with separately, while I counted our blessings that director Fred Fern was paying the players' wages out of his own pocket as we battled for survival. Now Maxwell wasn't so keen to climb into bed with us. "I cannot be seen to be associated with a company having writs served against it. You go off and sort yourselves out," he said to me, with the air of a man pulling on his trousers and shinning down a drainpipe.

Life on the pitch was increasingly messy, too, as defeats stacked up in a season of unremitting gloom, enlightened only by the FA Cup. Cambridge United and non-League Telford United were seen off before First Division Norwich City came a cropper at the Baseball Ground. Suddenly, Peter Taylor and the boys found themselves in the sixth round, facing a team in an even more parlous state. Bottom of Division Three entertained bottom of Division Two as Plymouth Argyle took on the Rams. A fortunate 0-0 draw in Devon meant a lucrative midweek replay four days later and the enticing prospect of a massive payday in the semi-final against Watford at Villa Park. Victory now in Derby's most pressing hour-and-a-half of need would be life-changing, like a tramp winning the Lotto jackpot.

I spent most of Wednesday, 14 March in London, trying to persuade Maxwell not to walk away, although within an hour of Justice Mervyn Davies, sitting in court 36 of the High Court, throwing out the club's proposed survival package, the tycoon had already prepared a statement to say he was no longer interested in Derby County.

As I boarded the train home from St Pancras that evening, I offered up a silent prayer for the team to win. God, how we deserved a break, didn't we? The journey was agonising, numerous scenarios playing out in my mind. But I clung to the

JUDGMENT DAY

belief that we would win, having done the hard work at Plymouth and beating a superior Norwich side in the fifth round. The moment I saw Josie's face when she came to pick me up from the station, I knew the outcome. She was crestfallen and so was I. Plymouth had won with a freak goal direct from an inswinging corner. So ended one of the most depressing days of my life.

John Kirkland told me he had spoken to Maxwell on the phone at half-time to relay the bad news that Derby were losing, to be asked: "What are you going to do about it?"

By Thursday morning, Derby was an unhappy city. The club was out of the FA Cup and looked to be going out of existence. Over the following weeks, the pressure was enormous with the club teetering on the brink of bankruptcy, and a fascinated Maxwell unable to quite sever his ties as he instigated cut-price offers in the High Court to try to satisfy the creditors.

Grim as it was, the situation was not without moments of black humour. On one occasion John Kirkland came down to London with several directors. When our solicitor asked the taxi driver to drop us in Carey Street, at the rear entrance to the High Court, John's eyebrows shot up as he sighed: "Carey Street? Bloody hell, Stuart, my heart sinks. That's the one place I vowed I would never end up."

Tom Pendry, Labour MP for Stalybridge and Hyde, now Lord Pendry and a Rams fan, wangled me a meeting at HM Treasury with John Moores, the then First Secretary and a keen footballer who played left-wing for the House of Commons team. He gave it to me straight: "Stuart, I have every sympathy with you and it would be a very sad day if Derby County cease to exist. But look at it this way – if the Inland Revenue or Customs and

Excise accept one penny less than they are due, it will open up a horrendous can of worms. I would have every business in the country wanting to use the precedent to wriggle out of repaying PAYE and VAT in full."

Back in the High Court, the patience of Mr Justice Davies – or "Merv the Swerve" as Gerald Mortimer dubbed him in the *Derby Evening Telegraph*, the same nickname given to his namesake Mervyn Davies, the Wales Rugby Union number eight – was wearing thin. I had been going there every fortnight seeking adjournments. After another of our jousts, he took off his spectacles, looked up to the roof in exasperation and told me: "Mr Webb, I don't want to see you in this courtroom again."

"Well, I need to be here," I pleaded, "because I need to know, can you give us, or can we spend, £500 for the reserve-team coach going to Stoke and Preston this week?"

"Yes, go on, then," he replied. "But that's all you're getting."

I was advised that not only were Derby County now on thin ice, it was starting to crack. The judge was convinced that we were merely delaying the "evil day". Happily, that day never arrived. After some frantic late-night negotiations, deals were done. A large proportion of creditors accepted an offer of 50 per cent, and I agreed the exact sums, with interest, that were due to the Inland Revenue and the VAT.

The decisive Inland Revenue v DCFC match in the High Court was scheduled for an 11am kick-off on Monday, 2 April 1984. I had lost count of the occasions I'd been to London and returned with our faithful solicitor, Arthur Willis, in a state of depression, alleviated on the journey home only by a few glasses of red wine to revive my defiance.

JUDGMENT DAY

Now I sunk a couple of cups of strong coffee on the 7am train to the capital. I was buzzing after arranging for a vital bank transfer of £127,000 to be collected from the Royal Bank of Scotland, situated in the Strand next door to the High Court. Willis went inside to reassure the Inland Revenue and Customs and Excise lawyers: "Your money is on the way."

But could I get them to release the money? It was a close-run thing. I had spent all week scraping the cash together – £25,000 from each of the five directors, myself included. £25,000 was a lot of money, not the sort of amount you could pull out of your back pocket, and it took a hell of a lot of co-ordination and chivvying to get the full £127,000 lodged in a Birmingham branch of the RBS by close of play on Thursday. Staff there assured me it would be a perfectly simple task to make a wire transfer to London. Had I known the aggravation awaiting me, I would have driven to Birmingham on Friday and picked up the draft personally. Still, I strode confidently into the bank in the Strand, saying words to the effect: "Stuart Webb, Derby County, I've come for my money," only to be met by indifference and apathy. Anything and everything appeared to be too much trouble.

I did my best to maintain my composure, but the staff with whom I was dealing were more interested in their first coffee of the working day than locating the missing draft. The hands on my watch were sprinting like Allan Wells towards 11am, and the back of my shirt was soaked in sweat. If I wasn't in the High Court with that draft in a matter of minutes, Derby County were going down and out, make no mistake about it. Everybody had had enough of us, the Inland Revenue, the VAT, the judge, everybody.

In desperation and frustration, I barged into the manager's office. I told him who I was and demanded that he instigate some action immediately to find the missing draft. I think the threat, "If Derby County go to the wall today, pal, I will drag your Royal Bank of Scotland through every 'effin court in Britain to get compensation," might have been uttered. "You've five minutes to find that draft – or else."

I ended up screaming down his phone to Birmingham, where a chap told me: "Oh! It's here, we're just getting round to it." I grabbed the draft, literally sprinting out of the bank and up the stairs of the central lobby to determine in which court my old sparring partner, Judge Mervyn Davies, would be sitting.

I spotted Arthur Willis in the corridor with the other lawyers. The four of us crammed into the gents' toilet where I handed over the bank transfer made out in full and final settlement to the Revenue and the Customs and Excise. I had a pee and washed my hands.

The implications of the agreement struck in the gents were relayed to Mr Justice Davies. "Very well," he said. "Lift the petition. No costs," to cheers from a group of Derby fans in the public gallery.

Arthur Willis later reflected:

> *There had been a lot of talking among the directors and the fans, but Stuart Webb was the only one to take action. He contacted me and a plan was formulated to stave off the inevitable, which was Derby County being kicked out of professional football. Had it not been for Stuart's determination to carry on the fight it would have been all*

over. We spent a lot of time together and his tenacity and quick grasp of the mountain of difficulties was paramount.

Stuart was tireless in his efforts and put in hours at meetings, travelling, attending conference and at court. On days when things had not gone well he was down for an hour, but over a glass of wine on the train back to Derby he was back and up again working out his plans for the next day's fight.

Without his effort and dedication I think the club would have folded. Others may have bought out bits from the liquidator but we would certainly not have had the Derby County Football Club that continued up to and well past its hundredth birthday. Not many people realise just how close Derby County were to extinction.

Dear old Arthur. He was Derby County's solicitor for many years, always available to give balanced and sound advice to the club and its directors. He was without doubt at his finest during that battle with the High Court in 1984. He was committed and totally supportive to the cause of keeping the Rams in business during the centenary year. He was a professional in every sense of the word. I was so very sad to learn of his passing in February 2016.

I still find it difficult to express the relief I experienced when the words "Lift the petition" were uttered. It felt as if I had conquered Everest. The club had made it. We'd been drinking in the last-chance saloon way past closing time but we were still in business. Yet it was a sombre gathering on the other side of the Strand, in the historic Wig and Pen Club, the haunt of lawyers and journalists. We had won a very famous victory but we didn't know where we were going, we didn't know what we were doing. We only knew that we'd just spent a lot of our own money.

Survival meant everything to men such as Geoff Glossop, who stayed on the board until 1991. He is a genuine fan who was never in the game to turn a profit and told a mutual friend:

> *I caught the Derby County 'bug' from my dad when I was six. Twenty-nine years and two league titles later, when Stuart Webb walked into my office and asked me to join the board, there was only one answer.*
>
> *A few days later I was invited to attend my first board meeting. Imagine my horror when the first item on the agenda was to consider placing the club into receivership because of its financial situation.*
>
> *Later that evening when I was dining out in Littleover, a bottle of aspirin appeared on my plate. It had been sent over by Stuart, who was also eating there.*
>
> *The next few months required many an aspirin, as we struggled to keep the club alive ... and now the 'bug' has been passed on to further generations, courtesy of my sons Guy and Jordan.*

Within 48 hours of the great escape, I took over from John Kirkland to become the club's sixth chairman in five years. Peter Taylor, meanwhile, left "by mutual consent". He was a broken man, and I thought it was thoroughly decent of him to accept a nominal pay-off in light of our financial difficulties. It was inaccurate to say Derby were going nowhere under Peter.

JUDGMENT DAY

We were going down at a rate of knots. Two of his last three results were a 3-0 home defeat by Brighton and a 5-1 humbling at Barnsley. Roy McFarland stepped up to take charge until the end of the campaign, but the die had been cast and nine years after being crowned champions of England, Derby County found themselves in the Third Division.

14

Captain Bob

"**P**UBLICITY?" Robert Maxwell confidently told me, "I'm up there with The Beatles and Presley." A physical giant of a man, he resembled nothing so much as a monstrous medieval king sitting on his throne as staff vetted those who required an audience, sometimes in a magnificent apartment furnished by Jon Bannenberg, the yacht designer. Immensely powerful and overbearing, Maxwell might keep you waiting for hours, some people for days. "You smell," he crushed one unfortunate visitor. "Would you care to leave my presence?" Responding meekly, the man said: "Sorry sir, but I have been waiting for a couple of days."

His vanity extended to having his mane of hair trimmed and dyed black – using L'Oreal Crescendo, I noticed – every fortnight by the Savoy Hotel's George Wheeler, his favourite barber, who visited Maxwell's penthouse and deployed the kitchen sink.

Maxwell spoke fluent Russian, Hebrew, English… and bullshit. If Brian Clough and Peter Taylor represented the Wild

CAPTAIN BOB

West, then Maxwell was the ringmaster of Barnum & Bailey, a figure deluded into thinking he was starring in *The Greatest Show on Earth*. He considered himself important, if not central, to anything and everything that captured his imagination. Cap'n Bob, RM, The Publisher or The Chairman, the man born plain Jan Ludvik Hoch, a Czechoslovakian Jew, manifested himself in any number of guises. In England, he became Du Maurier, which he considered classy as it was the brand of an upmarket cigarette he smoked, then Leslie Jones and eventually Ian Robert Maxwell, considered to have a dependable, solid, Scottish resonance which would be of benefit in business. We couldn't afford to be fussy – we needed to get him into the Baseball Ground under any name.

When Derby met Juventus in the European Cup semi-final in 1973, I experienced what Gianni Agnelli, the head of the Fiat empire, had achieved for the Italian club with his vast wealth. I sensed what could happen if a huge corporation took over a club, basically setting the purchase of star players against tax losses. So that was my model when I went to Maxwell. I said: "Look, the money you're making from the Mirror Group, Maxwell Communications etc, put that across to Derby County because Derby should be part of your empire and it's a tax write-off."

Actually, it would be 1987 before he became fully involved with Derby County. For now, though, he told me: "I want my son Ian to be the Derby chairman," and a spot of argy-bargy ensued as the other directors relayed the message back: "No, we're running a business and we know what we're doing." Maxwell got his wish, however, insisting I stay on as chief executive and deputy chairman to offer Ian guidance and stability. As chairman, Ian was extremely good to work with. When I asked him for something, it tended to get done although everything was channelled through Cap'n Bob. He was the guy who clearly said "yes" or "no" to transfers.

By the end of the 1983-84 season, with Derby County facing a future in the Third Division, I had pulled off a major coup by persuading Arthur Cox to resign from Newcastle United and become the Rams' new manager. It was only a matter of weeks since Newcastle, bound for promotion to the First Division, had thrashed us 4-0 on Tyneside with Kevin Keegan, Peter Beardsley and Chris Waddle running riot. Yet Cox was unimpressed with his proposed transfer budget for the following season, especially as Keegan had decided to hang up his boots.

I set up everything for Cox to come down on Monday, 28 May for a press conference the following day to confirm his appointment. My peace and sense of satisfaction on Sunday afternoon was shattered by a phone call. "Captain Bob here," said the voice on the other end of the line. "What are we going to do about a manager?"

I started to reply. "Well, we've got this press conference tomorrow …" but that was as far as I got before he interrupted to purr with satisfaction: "Good, you've got a press conference. And I'll be there with our new manager."

"What?" I cried in horror. "Yes," said Maxwell, "I'm bringing our new manager – The Bald Eagle." Jim Smith was the only manager Maxwell knew because he was at Oxford United. I said: "I'm sorry, Mr Maxwell, but we've got a manager, Arthur Cox, already set up." The revelation had Maxwell barking: "Who the fuck is Arthur Cox? Cox? Who is this man Cox? I'm the new owner and chairman – so listen up."

I contacted Ian Maxwell immediately, to warn him: "Look, there's a stand-off here. Your father doesn't want Arthur Cox at any price but this guy's already left his job, a big club at Newcastle, to come to us at Derby."

Like The Publisher, Ian was not totally au fait with football, the inside track, the knowledge that we had got a good gaffer in Cox, somebody who could handle himself and would be happy working in a club like Derby and get us back where we wanted to be. After I emphasised that Cox would have strong claims in court against Derby County for sharp practice if he was jilted, Ian managed to persuade his father to back off and leave Smith at Oxford. Over a decade later, I was delighted to welcome Jim to the Baseball Ground and we enjoyed six exciting years and promotion to the Premier League together, but in the summer of 1984 I felt Arthur was the perfect candidate to run the show on the pitch.

Maxwell was initially well received by the supporters, who were relieved the club's financial plight would be over, but Cox and several members of his managerial team were very unsure of his motives. An ardent self-publicist, Maxwell was here, there and everywhere. In team photographs, coming on to the pitch, all that sort of stuff – he loved it. It came as a surprise not to hear his name when the teams were read out.

Trying to patiently teach him how transfers were conducted was impossible. He had no idea how the market worked. I told him the value of a player and that Cox and I agreed it was a fair price, and Maxwell snorted with derision: "£500,000! Here, give me the phone. I'll speak to their chairman, we'll get him for

£300,000," and so he bullied and blustered on, only to be gently rebuffed: "Oh, I'm sorry, I don't get involved, Mr Maxwell. This is being done between my manager, my chief executive and your Mr Webb." Undeterred, Maxwell ploughed on: "Never mind Webb, I'm the boss," but the system defeated him totally. He could not comprehend that other chairmen were not hands-on and were not prepared to negotiate or fall under his spell.

* * * * *

Not long after Maxwell's takeover, I received a call from Jack Dunnett, president of the Football League and chairman of Notts County. "Stuart, you know Bob has bought the club?" he said. "I do, Jack," I replied. "I did the deal." It was just what he wanted to hear. "Good, now I want you to come down and see me at the House of Commons. Bob and I would like to think about merging Derby County with Notts County." I couldn't quite believe what I was hearing. "Oh, yeah?" I said, buying time. "Yes," he went on. "We think it would be great for our clubs."

Maxwell had wanted to merge Oxford United and Reading to create Thames Valley Royals, that was his dream, and now here he was, cooking up the idea of joining Derby County and Notts County. It was ridiculous, but the trouble was he was colluding with the president of the Football League, a man who would have had no trouble getting the proposed merger rubber-stamped – if they could get it that far – and a man who could see how it would get Notts County out of a mess. And they were in one, all right, because they were going nowhere.

I said: "Jack, listen. After all I've been through these past three months trying to save the club, I'm not going to give it

CAPTAIN BOB

away now." He hit back: "Well, Bob wants to do it. We should conduct a feasibility study." I met Jack at his house in Nottingham and impressed upon him that it wouldn't get off the ground. They wanted to amalgamate the fans. Amalgamate the fans? No wonder: Notts County only had 3,000 of them. It was very serious, but I went back to Maxwell and told him there was no way it would happen, that I'd walk out of the door, that I hadn't saved the club just to merge it with Notts County. Thankfully, for once, he listened.

* * * * *

Arthur Cox worked wonders in getting Derby County promoted in successive seasons, but at the start of the 1987-88 campaign he had a nagging fear that we lacked the defensive efficiency and nous to survive in the First Division without high-class reinforcements. Until now, the most we had ever paid for a player was £410,000 to bring in centre-forward David Swindlehurst in April 1980 when punters joked that he was likely to be more of a swindle than a Hurst on the evidence of signings made by the previous manager, Tommy Docherty.

Maxwell pushed the boat out to take the England goalkeeper, Peter Shilton, off Southampton's hands on a huge salary, and while we were dealing with the Saints, I sensed we had half a chance of getting his club and country team-mate, Mark Wright, too. Cox was excited by the prospect, even though we knew the centre-half was an expensive option. Still, negotiations progressed between the south coast and the East Midlands to the point where Wright was almost in the bag with Southampton accepting our offer of £760,000. And that's when the trouble started. Maxwell insisted Wright "couldn't play" and snapped at me: "What are you signing him for?" Little did I know, but our overlord didn't have enough money to complete the transfer.

Cox and I decided Wright was going to come regardless and started talking wages with him. Maxwell knew nothing about football but he loved to convey the impression that he had his finger on the pulse, having been briefed by the *Daily Mirror*'s chief football writer, Harry Harris, and assorted hangers-on, who would manufacture any old line to ingratiate themselves with Cap'n Bob, owner of Derby County Football Club. In his own warped world, Maxwell became an aficionado of football, convinced he knew everything that was going on. "Wright?" he scoffed. "He'll fail his medical. I've heard he's injury prone."

We shocked the football world by jumping in to do the deal with Southampton. It was a huge coup because several big clubs – Kenny Dalglish's Liverpool, and Sheffield Wednesday among them – were primed to strike for Wright. He had just turned 24 and had won 16 England caps. His potential was massive, but we had him, I felt sure.

We got Wright to Derby, agreed personal terms, settled everything. But we couldn't get the money out of Maxwell. He was on his new luxury yacht, the *Lady Ghislaine*, and was proving strangely elusive. Not unreasonably, our new centre-half wanted to know what he was supposed to be doing – when he was putting pen to paper; the timing of the press conference to announce his signing – and the best I could do was employ stalling tactics. I got my assistant, Michael Dunford, to take him to Allestree and show him a few houses, purely to get him out the way and give me some breathing space. I'm working

CAPTAIN BOB

on Maxwell, trying all the numbers I knew to get in touch, and Cox is demanding to know: "What the bloody hell's happening? When are we signing him?"

Eventually, I manufactured some cock-and-bull story that seemed to satisfy Wright, and booked him an overnight stay in a nice hotel. That evening Harry Harris rang me: "What's going on? Bob's anxious, I want to do the best for Bob." I told the *Mirror* man: "Look Harry, off the record, the deal is more or less done. The player is not going to Liverpool, he's not going here, he's not going there. Mark Wright is in Derby and it's only a matter of time before we'll have him and we'll give you a shout then. I'll let you know. We're working on it."

Of course, Harry puts it in the *Mirror* and the next morning their back-page headline screams: 'Derby sign Wright.' Maxwell, still on his boat in the bloody Mediterranean, insisted on getting the *Mirror* pages faxed through to him and he went absolutely ballistic, screaming down the phone: 'You've got to put the money in. If you sign him, you put the money in. I'm not putting in a penny.'

Dunford came to my rescue the following morning and volunteered to take Wright off to see yet more houses, this time in Oakwood, another suburb, but now the transfer was not so much smelling of fish, but stinking of the rotten stuff. Cox is pacing around, a bear with a sore head, other clubs are convinced that we are fatally wounded, can't close the deal, and start circling like sharks. It is all going wrong, belly-up, the player is becoming frustrated, and Maxwell still offers no encouragement: "This Wright fellow needs to see a top specialist in London. I'm not paying for him to play for Derby County and that's final." I pleaded: "Look, Mr Maxwell, if we sign him he will have to undergo a medical and we'll have the best doctors available. We'll even send him to Harley Street if you want – and we won't sign him unless he's fully fit."

Time was running out. People were looking at their watches and tapping their feet impatiently. With Maxwell's cheque book defiantly closed, I had a sinking feeling that another star player was slipping away, like Storey-Moore did. My four fellow directors and I each put in £20,000. We got enough for a hundred grand deposit. I negotiated extended terms so we didn't pay Southampton £760,000 up front. I budgeted that we could cover the scheduled payments out of our cash flow. Season-ticket money was rolling in, attendances would be higher in the First Division. We were covered.

As the much-delayed press conference was announced to unveil Wright as our player, I had Maxwell screaming over the phone: "Take this statement down." I felt confident that I'd got him onside at last and that he would dictate a quote to the press, hijacking all the prestige from signing an England international. "Take this statement down … I, Stuart Webb, hereby resign my position …" and there I was, writing it down, like a prat. Unbelievable.

Maxwell did everything to block the transfer but Wright passed a stringent medical with flying colours. As for being an injury risk, he made his debut at home against Wimbledon and was ever-present for the rest of the season. He successfully played more than 170 times for Derby County, and went to the World Cup in Italy in 1990 before we finally sold him to Liverpool for £2.5million. He finished with 45 England caps, not bad going for a player who Maxwell said "couldn't play".

CAPTAIN BOB

❈ ❈ ❈ ❈ ❈

Towards the end of 1987, Maxwell was playing silly beggars again. Cox was out training one Friday morning when I received a call from London. "Where are you?" demanded the familiar voice.

"I'm at the ground."

"Right, I want you on the 12 o'clock train and in my office by two-thirty. Where's Cox?"

"He's training, it's Friday morning and there's a big game tomorrow."

"OK, bring him with you. I want you down in my office, urgently. Both of you."

When I phoned Cox with the news the manager was apoplectic: "For fuck's sake, Stuart, you can't disturb me on a Friday. I'm with the players. You know what it's like. I'm not going, Maxwell's a berk."

"Well, I'm going on the 12 o'clock train, Arthur, See you on the platform. If you're not there, I'll explain to the chairman that you're busy."

When I reached the station, Cox met me, booted and suited. Down we went, Arthur grumbling every mile of the way. A beaming Maxwell burst into the room where we were awaiting his presence, wondering why on earth we had been summoned, and thrust a sheet of paper at each of us.

Cox and I studied a typed list of players, Watford players, as Maxwell, uncharacteristically agreeable for once, asked: "Can you please put your value on those players?" before departing to attend to other guests.

When the nature of his business trip became apparent, Cox started moaning, shouting the odds again.

"Arthur, just get on with it," I said. "The sooner we finish, the sooner we're out of this place."

And so we got on with deciding how much Dave Bassett's team, including Luther Blissett, Kenny Jackett and Iwan Roberts, might fetch in the transfer market. I put a figure against the Watford goalkeeper, Tony Coton. Cox leant over to see what I had written and I warned: "No conferring!" "Fuck off, Webby," he roared as we doubled-up with laughter. It was a ridiculous scenario. The Derby County manager and chief executive hauled away from important work to travel 120 miles to help the owner buy another club. Maxwell wanted Cox's expertise in the transfer market, and mine, but it was nothing to do with Derby County.

The Watford owner, Elton John, and chief executive, Eddie Plumley, nodded hurriedly to us as they emerged from another room before scuttling away. Maxwell was negotiating a price for Watford and was eager to factor the club's playing assets into the equation before he made an offer. When Maxwell reappeared to send us on our way, the growling Cox had disappeared, to be replaced by a pussycat, but all the way home to Derby he was preparing and rehearsing his excuses for the following afternoon's defeat. Of course we lost, and the manager made sure that the press knew that it was down to Cap'n Bob, me, and the administration, rather than to any deficiency in tactics or lack of football nous on Arthur's part. Cox was damned if he was going to be left carrying the can.

In November 1987, Elton John tried to sell his controlling interest in Watford to Maxwell for £2million, but the Football League blocked the move and brought in a rule preventing the major shareholder of any member club from owning more than two per cent of another League team. Maxwell was permitted to keep his stakes in Derby and Oxford – not to mention Reading and his misguided vision for Thames Valley Royals – but Watford was out of bounds.

* * * * *

Harold Wilson famously said: "A week is a long time in politics," but I needed the diplomatic skills of another noted mover and shaker, Henry Kissinger, to prevent a nasty bout of infighting in April 1988, during a week I thought would never end. We fielded a call from the *Daily Mirror* to say that Johan Cruyff was arriving at Derby as technical director, that Maxwell had brokered a deal through some politician who knew the great Dutchman. It was all going to happen, it was all very serious. Maxwell wanted it. He craved the publicity, the showbusiness element. And he also wanted something to happen because he felt that Arthur Cox wasn't doing it. A dismal sequence of eight successive League defeats between mid-December and the middle of February had seen Derby plunge down the table.

Maxwell wanted a big name to lift the club – a little like Manchester United with José Mourinho – and he was in daily dialogue with Cruyff, the *Mirror* quick to print a picture of the two shaking hands. People he courted would be flown over to London, waited on hand and foot in a penthouse suite, go to see Maxwell and, in Cruyff's case, tell Cap'n Bob about how he nearly won the World Cup for Holland in 1974 and was considering his options after coaching Ajax to win the European Cup-winners' Cup and introducing such likely lads as Frank Rijkaard, Arnold Muhren, Dennis Bergkamp and Marco van Basten.

CLOUGH, MAXWELL & ME

I spent days on the phone to Maxwell, saying: "I don't think this is a good thing. We're not going to be able to buy superstars. We've no money in the budget for major signings. Cruyff will want to bring ten new players with him, and Diego Maradona will be one of them. It won't work."

In Derby's odd-jobbing team that was scrapping to maintain a foothold in the First Division were a couple of players I don't think Cruyff would relish training. I had to explain to Maxwell the gap between Cruyff's pedigree and the current state of our side. And also how any link between Cruyff and Cox would work – or rather, how it wouldn't work. If Cruyff had brought his boots, it might have been better. To come as technical director, some sort of super coach, was a recipe for disaster.

I told Maxwell that we were digging a hole for ourselves because I could see that Cox would walk away carrying a good legal case that we had forced him out. I attempted to balance the whole thing in a way that would placate Maxwell's ego while not infuriating him into doing something rash and jeopardising the future of the club. He sulked, moaning: "You think you know best," and put the phone down on me, effin' and blinding.

In the week "Cruyff for Derby" had a life of its own, Cox would not have been human had he not been distracted by the speculation and we suffered damaging defeats: 1-0 at Chelsea and 2-0 at home to Queens Park Rangers. When Cruyff announced at the end of the week that he would become Barcelona coach for a year, declining the offer from Derby, I was delighted. Next time we spoke, I said to Maxwell: "Well, I think we've done the right thing." He simply ignored my comments and swore at me again. He could never admit that he was in the wrong, and there

CAPTAIN BOB

was never, ever a pat on the back. Johan Cruyff at the Baseball Ground? It would have been like trying to get Madonna in for a turn at the Wheeltappers' and Shunters' social club.

* * * * *

One year on from the Wright move, with myself and the other directors reimbursed by Maxwell, Cox was in the hunt for a top-class striker and told me he fancied Dean Saunders at Oxford United. I took a sharp intake of breath because that meant business between two clubs controlled by Maxwell. Kevin Maxwell was Oxford chairman in name, but a puppet in reality with Cap'n Bob pulling the strings at the Manor Ground. The fee for the Wales international was £1million. The money had to be seen to change hands and arrive in Oxford's bank account, so the transfer was carefully arranged between the Football League and myself. There had to be absolute transparency. I even went to the League and said: "You have to manage this properly because people will ask questions. Did Saunders come for nothing? Was there a deal done?" I didn't want any muck-raking or mud-slinging at Derby County.

I sympathised with the Oxford manager, Mark Lawrenson. He had been in his first job on the other side of the fence for seven months after enjoying a fabulous playing career at a great club, Liverpool, where good players routinely arrived rather than left. When told Saunders to Derby was a done deal, Lawrenson turned round and said simply: "This can't happen." I heard that Maxwell's response was: "It can because I am in charge and you can get back to work on the training ground." That's how he talked to people. Lawrenson was dead set against the transfer on a matter of principle and he became a dead man walking when he blew his top and told Maxwell he could stuff his job. Lawrenson went into his office the following day to draft a letter of resignation, only to find he'd been beaten to the punch. Maxwell had sacked him.

* * * * *

Allowed to land his helicopter on the roof of the *Mirror* building in busy Holborn Circus, Maxwell would go to the edge and pee into the street blow. He said that the City had pissed on him long enough, now he was getting even. I made sure I wasn't walking below when he'd just landed. Unsuspecting passers-by just marvelled at the cloudless sky.

Maxwell recruited Peter Jay, the former British ambassador in Washington, as his chief of staff. Jay was reputed to be the "cleverest man in England". I sometimes popped into his office for a chat or a glass of wine: Jay enjoyed a bottle of Mouton Cadet with lunch. One day I was in the White Hart – known as the "Stab in the Back" because it was a venue for the darkest office politics.

It was the favourite Fleet Street haunt of *Mirror* people and it was there that I heard the story of Jay going into the newsroom with a chart setting out his plans for reorganising working days and the holiday roster – no mean task because those hard-nosed journalists didn't like change. From the back of the room one angry sub-editor called out: "Hey! Mr Jay … you're supposed to be the cleverest man in the whole of England. How come you didn't wear a johnny when you fucked the nanny." (Jay had had an affair with his children's nanny, who bore him a son.) It brought the house down, and the meeting more or less ended there.

15

Bouncing Czechs

THE NAMES Lubos Kubik and Ivo Knoflicek still make me shift uneasily in my seat, bringing back memories of some of my most uncomfortable days at the Baseball Ground.

How the two Czech internationals were spirited away to Derby County in 1989, yet never kicked a ball in anger for the club, remains a huge mystery, containing elements of a spy thriller. The plot might have been developed into a John le Carré novel.

I took a call from Robert Maxwell, ordering me to stand by for a visit from "Bond", who was a friend of his, and another acquaintance, prominent Conservative Jonathan Guinness, a member of the famous Guinness brewing dynasty.

"What's it all about, Mr Chairman?" I enquired.

"Two new players, you'll find out soon enough," he told me with a sense of smug self-satisfaction. "This is good business for the club."

CLOUGH, MAXWELL & ME

Whatever qualities Guinness possessed, as far as I knew a detailed knowledge of the workings of the football transfer market was not among them. We didn't need a faceless middleman to conduct our business professionally. Arthur Cox identified potential signings and, if they fell within Maxwell's price range, I did my best to get them over the line. Now my heart sank; already I had a gnawing sense that this was not going to end well.

Guinness duly arrived with a swarthy East European "Mister Fixit", the sort of character you might expect to find in a movie; certainly not one to put you at your ease. I was briefed: That July, two Slavia Prague players – Kubik, 24, a midfielder, and Knoflicek, 26, a winger – had absconded from a training camp during a pre-season tournament in West Germany and were seeking asylum in the West — these were, remember, still the days of the Iron Curtain. Maxwell was going to offer them this great opportunity at Derby County. "Mister Fixit" wanted me to work with him to make it happen because Maxwell had told him that, as managing director, I was the man with whom he must deal.

I learned that Kubik and Knoflicek had been smuggled by British agents into Belgium, where they were holed up for a couple of weeks. It was at this stage that Maxwell ordered Cox and myself to greet the players, so we flew to Brussels and arrived at a typical, nondescript airport hotel. There we met "Mister Fixit" who did the introductions while "Bond" assured them they would be warmly welcomed by the Rams and our fans. So far, so good. However, Kubik and Knoflicek became nervous when they spotted several mysterious guests arriving in the lobby with bulging muscles and shoulder holsters poking out of their dark suit jackets. The nerves soon spread.

BOUNCING CZECHS

Cox and I took one look at the assembled team of heavies, any one of whom made Oddjob from the film *Goldfinger* look positively anaemic, and decided to retreat to our rooms pronto, taking the stairs five at a time. "Don't use the lifts," barked Arthur. "They'll trap us."

I was shattered now, mentally and physically, and about to turn in for the night when there was a knock on my door and Arthur arrived, his brow furrowed. "Listen," he hissed. "I'm not happy with this situation. Those two lads appear OK, but we're in the middle of a major bloody diplomatic incident here. We're going to have to scarper first thing in the morning … and while you're at it, double lock the door, and stick a chair and a wardrobe behind it."

Talk about drama. "You've been watching too many thrillers," I told him but Arthur was deadly serious and said with a worried look on his face: "I signed a contract with Derby County Football Club … not MI5!"

We didn't sleep well, got up at the crack of dawn and without saying farewell to assorted parties – especially those guys packing pistols – caught the first available flight back to East Midlands Airport.

Quite apart from those heavies, Czech Football Association officials had arrived in Belgium to convince the pair to return, but they refused before being moved to Holland and shipped out to Portugal, where they went into hiding. The players, I was told, were eager for freedom from the restrictions of life behind the Iron Curtain, and the opportunity to earn big money, but the Czech authorities would sanction such transfers only for players over the age of 30. Did they decide to fall out of Czech control, or were they pushed? I didn't know the identities of the prime movers here, and I never did find out.

Josie and I were invited to a New Year's Eve bash at Osbaston Hall, then Jonathan Guinness's 18th-century, 14-bedroom country house in Leicestershire, where I was to receive further instructions on where to find the players again. The party was a who's who of society: 30 or so people in dinner jackets, evening dress, naval uniform. I sensed that deals were being brokered all over the place among the large cigars, flutes of champagne and genteel chitter-chatter to the accompaniment of classical music. It was almost MI5 stuff, what you might expect to see in a James Bond movie. And there I was in the middle of it, not really knowing which way to turn or what I was supposed to be doing.

I wondered what government regulations Derby County were poised to break. I knew that we were on dodgy ground with FIFA and UEFA because Kubik and Knoflicek were registered Czech FA internationals under contract to Slavia Prague. We would have one hell of a job getting round those obstacles before Cox could parade them in the First Division. And there, at the back of my mind, was the fear that kidnapping might be involved; that they had not instigated the drama. I considered the middlemen or minders to be spies, whose interest was purely financial. They were keen to clinch the deal and disappear, but not before being paid off by Maxwell or the club for providing players worth a very tidy sum on the open market.

This time I tracked down Kubik and Knoflicek to the Guinness's 18th-century former monastery in Cadaques, on the Spanish coast near Barcelona, where the neighbours included Salvador Dali, and I found them keeping fit by playing tennis when they weren't kicking their heels in frustration. "What are we doing? When are we coming to Derby?" they wanted to know. They were reasonable queries.

Back in England, I went to the Football Association, applied for this, applied for that. The FA was adamant: No, they couldn't do it. Kubik and Knoflicek were registered players with another club in another country. Derby needed proof positive from Slavia Prague and the Czech authorities that the transfers had been completed in good faith. Maxwell, appalled that his masterplan to recruit a couple of leading European players for peanuts had hit the buffers, ordered me to approach the Government. No joy there either. It was a tedious job. I felt like an idiot, going cap-in-hand to people who must have thought that I, personally, had lost the plot.

Josie was busy buying tracksuits and other gear at His and Hers in Derby, Marks & Spencer and Next to send to the players, anything to keep them sweet. And it was a mess, one hell of a mess.

I questioned why we were still involved, still trying to pull it off, when everything was stacked against us. The response from Maxwell was consistent: "Make it work, Webb. It's your job to make it work."

I flew to Barcelona on half-a-dozen missions, hiring a car to drive up the coast to try to reassure the players. They were political gypsies, refugees as such. Penniless and in limbo. The Czech Government was looking for them, their national team and Slavia were pissed off, and there they were under a spotlight with Derby County's name and fingerprints all over the shop. It was quite scary.

They were two human beings who hadn't got a house or a home and were missing their families. They had abandoned security, walked out with the promise of great riches in the West. I felt a sense of responsibility because Derby County – in the shape of Robert Maxwell – was part of that and I couldn't see an answer because in football law you simply can't sign another club's player without that club's agreement. We knew all that – simple facts. From Maggie Thatcher's point of view, would her Government let in someone who had walked out, claiming to be an asylum seeker? We didn't know that.

It was a massive gamble by Maxwell, and I was in the middle, talking to people I didn't know, certainly didn't trust, about trying to get two players, who were obviously excellent footballers, into England. And at the same time they were getting increasingly unsettled, wanting to know when they were arriving. Kubik insisted: "We've been promised this." And they had been promised the earth, they had been promised they could walk into England and would be playing for Derby County within three weeks, and seeing themselves on *Match of the Day* on a Saturday night against Liverpool, Arsenal and Manchester United.

As managing director, it was dropped into my lap because I was the guy holding their files, talking to the FA and the Government and seeking joy there in vain. I was also the guy talking to the players because the middlemen, having persuaded them to defect, were telling the Czech stars: "The club will sort it. You'll soon be getting your £20,000 a year."

The minders were always there in the background, a lurking presence, yet they were doing nothing because they couldn't do anything whatsoever. The players were left under the auspices of the Guinness family, who had the premises and the staff, but the middlemen were around, they were watching for any developments. To these guys, the players were pieces of meat. When we eventually took the plunge and brought them over to England, Maxwell typically made a big deal out of being pictured in the *Daily Mirror* with his "new signings". In January 1989, Maxwell, at a London press conference, introduced them as Derby County players.

We tried this, we tried that to force the issue but the Government didn't want to know, the FA didn't want to know. Nobody wanted to know. In fact, people were saying: "What are you doing with these bloody players at Derby? What are you trying to do?" What was clear to me was that I was the patsy. I could see no way of getting out of it, no way for the club to benefit, no way of Maxwell being happy with the outcome. I was running around like a blue-arsed fly, knowing in my heart of hearts that nothing would come of it.

One of the lads did play in a reserve match, but the situation was a mess, a cesspit, and very depressing for me because I was trying to hold it all together. I was trying to maintain my reputation and that of the club. I was trying to keep morale up, trying to do my best for the club and the owner at the same time, warning him: "Do you know what you're doing?"

Typical Maxwell, he thought he could bully people into getting the result he wanted. If he could get two stars to Derby for nothing, bulldoze it through by sheer force of personality, all well and good.

He failed totally to appreciate that while you are perfectly at liberty to take on the Government, you can't seriously expect to win in a situation such as this, and neither will you beat the FA, UEFA and FIFA when the rules are unambiguous in matters of players registered in another country with another club.

Once in England, my problem pair were lodged with Roger Pearman, the former Derbyshire cricket chief executive, who ran the Clovelly Hotel, before they moved into accommodation above an Italian restaurant, which we thought might be a touch more homely. They both impressed in training but Cox, despite being under orders from Maxwell to get the duo match-fit, wanted nothing to do with them because, like me, he knew they would never play for Derby unless Maxwell did a deal with the Czech authorities and agreed to pay Slavia Prague a respectable fee, options the Rams' owner was not prepared to consider. The club had already spent a sizeable amount of cash on the madcap scheme and, fixed resolutely in his mind, was the notion that Derby were getting two high-class performers for free.

On one hand some of the directors, who were not fully in the picture, and Cox were telling Maxwell: "Superb business, Mr Chairman, aren't you wonderful? The club's fortunes will be transformed by these two." His programme notes welcomed them to the club with a prescient rider: "There are still i's to be dotted and t's to be crossed before they are eligible to play competitively in any of our teams." But to my face, Cox complained: "Bloody hell, Stuart, we don't want these. What a load of rubbish, I'm not bothering with them."

When they were introduced to the Baseball Ground crowd before the Southampton FA Cup tie in January 1989, they were greeted with thunderous applause. They were all right as individuals, and more than that as top-class players, of course, but they were gypsies. They wanted a better life, and were sold a dream that turned into a nightmare. Kubik and Knoflicek's departure proved much swifter than their laboured arrival. I turned up for work one day to be informed they had returned to Prague to face the music. In June 1989, Italian club Fiorentina paid about £500,000 for the rights to Kubik, while Knoflicek went to Germany to sign for St Pauli in Hamburg. The following September, the whole unsavoury episode was front-page news in the *News of the World*, owned by Maxwell's arch-rival, Rupert Murdoch.

* * * * *

While Arthur Cox and members of his staff had questioned the chairman's motives for buying Derby County from the moment he walked through the door at the Baseball Ground, the supporters had initially given him their backing. They were delighted that someone had come in and invested in their club after seeing it so very nearly go to the wall, and they saw only a bright future – at the very least, a future – ahead. The goodwill, however, did not last.

Maxwell Communications had become our main sponsor but as Maxwell's standing with the fans deteriorated we decided to take the company logo off the replica jerseys we stocked in the Ramtique, the club shop.

A lot of fans refused to buy the shirts because they bore Maxwell's name, although the reason we actually stripped it off had nothing to do with any loss of revenue. It was purely because Maxwell feared that when his relationship with the supporters finally hit rock bottom – and it was hovering ominously close to that point – that there would be pictures of shirts being burnt in the streets and he realised the publicity would have backfired on him and reflected extremely badly on his company. He didn't want his name to be blackened. He was such an egotist and once something was going down, he cut it off.

* * * * *

Maxwell exuded power, magnetism and personality, and when he walked into a room everything seemed to stop. He had that sort of charisma, the same as Brian Clough in his heyday. He could be equally charming or venomous when he wanted. His temper was always on a short fuse and his blood pressure went up when restrictions were imposed on how often he could land his helicopter on the roof of the *Mirror* building in Holborn. To circumvent the law, something that came as second nature, The Publisher ordered his pilot to hover a few feet above the building before he jumped down. All was well until Maxwell came a cropper, finished up with his ankle in plaster and requiring the assistance of a walking stick.

One summer Saturday morning I was at Headington Hall to complete some paperwork when Maxwell summoned me in to what I took to be a private meeting with a Mirror Group senior executive, a nice guy. I was embarrassed because they were discussing insurance in a business that was no concern of mine. The executive had fallen foul of Maxwell, who started ranting and raving, before rising to his feet and bringing his stick down with an almighty crash, leaving an ugly indentation on the beautiful, polished boardroom table. The object of Maxwell's anger jumped out of his skin before being shown the door. Three months later that nice guy died from a heart attack.

BOUNCING CZECHS

I think Maxwell liked me because I stood up to him. My knowledge of football also made me useful. He bought my Lonsdale Travel business because he wanted me to be part of his wider empire. Lonsdale handled all the *Mirror*'s travel arrangements, and one Christmas, I got a call from Maxwell, who demanded: "Where's my bloody editor?" The journalist in question had sworn me to secrecy over plans to take a holiday in Barbados. Credit Maxwell, when it came to getting what he wanted, he was in a class of his own. He dispatched one of his lackeys from London to Derby specifically to interrogate the Lonsdale girl responsible for the booking. The editor was traced to his hotel in the Caribbean and told to be on the next available flight home or there would be no job for him. Bullying and pressure were facts of life under the publishing tycoon. Fortunately, before the Mirror Group became engulfed in a pensions scandal, together with Josie and John Cheadle I succeeded in buying back Lonsdale Travel, and I went on to build a substantial travel group in Derby that I eventually sold to Capita Group PLC. Over the years Josie combined her role as a director of Lonsdale with that of a local magistrate.

I once had to drive Maxwell to East Midlands Airport at the end of a game and, yet again, he was in a terrible mood. "Put the radio on," he barked as he climbed in. He wanted BBC Radio Derby on so he could hear what the fans were singing and the commentary team was saying about him. Maxwell was the worst passenger at the best of times. "Put your foot down, overtake him, speed up."

So I turned the radio on, looking for Radio Derby, but I didn't know the frequency. I'm panicking, moving the dial left to right with all the fuzz and interference winding Maxwell up to boiling point. "Get. The. Local. Fucking. Station. On." I'm trying to drive and fiddle with the radio at the same time, while he's to my left, seething, with steam coming out of his ears. He's telling me to drive through red lights, to go left, go right and I can feel myself breaking out in a sweat. Finally, I found it – Medium Wave, 1116kHz – and Maxwell's attention turned to the radio. He didn't speak to me again until we got to the airport, where he got out of the car, spun furiously on his heels to face me again, jammed his head back in through the open passenger door and roared, "You won't fucking forget that again, will you? You cunt!" Bang! He slammed the door. And he was right, I never did.

* * * * *

A paltry attendance of 12,469 for Wimbledon at home when the 1990-91 season kicked off was the beginning of the end for Maxwell, who had frequently maintained that he wanted to see crowds averaging 20,000 and more at the Baseball Ground – or else! He duly put the club up for sale at £8million. At that time football wasn't sexy, there was too much hooliganism and violence, and the Hillsborough disaster was uncomfortably fresh in everybody's mind. Supporters were turned off and Derby were far from alone in suffering at the turnstiles. Another First Division fixture, Queens Park Rangers versus Luton Town, realised an attendance of only 10,565.

Maxwell was having to put into Derby money that he didn't have. We didn't know it at the time, but his businesses were haemorrhaging money generally. The club was £2million in debt and the lack of investment in the playing staff became chronic,

BOUNCING CZECHS

while on the terraces the mood towards the owner became hostile, particularly during a calamitous 7-1 home defeat by Liverpool in March 1991. Arsenal were in town the following Saturday and soon on their way to a 2-0 win, while I sat next to Maxwell on the front row of the directors' box. The hardcore Derby fans away to our left on the Osmaston End were soon pointing and gesticulating at the owner as well as chanting his name in an offensive ditty.

The words "big, fat, ugly and bastard" were used, and references to him being a tightwad were clear to all and sundry, but Maxwell's hearing must have been faulty because he half-turned to me and beamed: "Listen, they're chanting my name," before waving to the angry fans. I reflected on his early days at the club when one banner hanging from a stand at the Baseball Ground read: "Robert Maxwell Walks On Water." How ironic was that, given his ultimate demise?

Anyway, half-time arrived and there were no more than seven of us in the cramped boardroom enjoying a cup of tea when the Arsenal vice-chairman, David Dein, casually wandered over and asked: "Why is it the fans don't like Bob? Why don't they respect him for what he has done for the club?" I shot David a glance but his voice had obviously carried in the confined space because Maxwell picked up on the mention of his name. While the others went for a pee, he interrogated me. "We were just discussing the fans, Chairman, nothing to concern you," I said.

We went out for the second half, Maxwell with a face like thunder, listening intently. The abuse rolled towards him again ... and that was it. He glared at me and said: "They are chanting my name, Webb, but that's not what I want to hear." I thought about telling him that he was mistaken, that they were chanting: "Maxwell is a banker." But he stood up, making a big, sweeping gesture, wrapped a camel coat around his shoulders and said: "I will never come back to this ground again. If they don't want me, they won't have me. I'm off. The club is up for sale tomorrow morning."

That started the process of Maxwell severing his ties with Derby County. He realised that the situation had turned massively against him. He wanted only glory; he wanted glamour. That's why he was an MP and why he owned a newspaper. Football gave him a platform. He elbowed his way past me, walked down the steps and out of the front entrance of the main stand. His helicopter was parked 200 yards away on a patch of green – and he never did come back.

* * * * *

Like many people stunned by tragic events, I can instinctively recall where I was the moment I heard of the Munich Air Disaster, the assassination of JFK, and Princess Diana's death. However, neither memories are as vivid as the one that whisks me back to Wilmorton College in Derby, where I was chairing a meeting of the board of governors, on 5 November 1991 – a date forever etched into my brain.

At around 4pm, a secretary tiptoed into the room and quietly informed me that a BBC Radio Derby reporter was in reception, urgently requesting to speak to me in relation to Robert Maxwell.

My initial reaction was: "Bloody hell, what has the old sod done now?" I excused myself from the meeting and set off to find out.

BOUNCING CZECHS

The bare facts were related to me: Maxwell had been aboard his yacht, the *Lady Ghislaine*, off Tenerife, and was reportedly missing at sea. A microphone was thrust under my nose ... would I care to comment?

My brain was running at 100mph, wondering how best to react. Was Maxwell dead? Had the coastguard found a body? And, if so, what were the implications, if any, for Derby County? How could I possibly react properly without knowing all the answers? Over the course of the next few days, it was confirmed that Cap'n Bob was indeed dead.

I won't pretend working with him involved much sweetness and light, at times he drove me to distraction, but he had been a massive character, playing a huge part in my life, and I was saddened to learn of his fate.

Not so many of the fans at the Baseball Ground, though. The minute's silence to mark his death a fortnight later, ahead of a 1-0 win over Ipswich, was seriously hostile as supporters booed loudly and chanted some pretty vile stuff about the club's former owner.

That was indicative of how sour the mood had turned towards Maxwell. The feelgood factor on his arrival had lasted about a year, but once Derby had been promoted, and Maxwell took over as chairman, he interfered too much. Once the fans realised that he was no longer willing to seriously finance new signings, they turned on him, as did the local press with Neil Hallam, in the *Derby Trader*, in particular questioning Maxwell's involvement with Derby County, and his motives for it.

Although he was vilified and became a cartoonish figure of hate, we should not forget that Maxwell stepped into the breach directly after our High Court victory, and he initially pumped money into the club.

That financial injection enabled the board and myself to set about building a structure for two successive promotions. There were days of wine and roses, before the sour grapes.

There will always be those who criticise Robert Maxwell for what he did at Derby County but the fact remains that when the club was on the brink of collapse nobody, no business, nor local council, came forward to help. But Maxwell did, investing in the club following the High Court victory. No matter what happened in the years that followed, without him there would have been no new stadium, no promotions to the Premier League, or Premiership as it was then known, no trips to Wembley. Simply, no club, and I know I was right to bring him in. But in the end, supporters wanted him gone, and when he set sail on that ill-fated trip around the Canary Islands they got their wish – albeit in slightly more final circumstances than I guess most of them really wanted, for all those cruel songs on the terraces.

Was it suicide, heart failure, an accident or murder? Did he jump or was he pushed? Speculation into Robert Maxwell's death continues to this day with no end of wild theories. Almost as many as there are about the true identity of Jack the Ripper. Amateur sleuths tell me that he was running out of cash, that he had Mafia connections, that he was a master spy for Mossad, the Israeli intelligence agency, that he was executed by a KGB hit squad or by the Bulgarian secret police.

Having known the man for several years and seen him operate at close quarters, I never believed that he would take his own life. He was too massively confident in his own ability to escape trouble. After all, he had survived many crises from his early days as plain Ludvik Hoch in the Eastern Bloc. The captain of the *Lady Ghislaine*, Gus Rankin, and his crew, who accompanied Maxwell on his last voyage, were perhaps better placed than anyone else to understand what happened that night, but in the past 25 years there have been few public utterances from any of those individuals.

16

The Name's Cox, Arthur Cox

MAYBE I was looking for perfection, or simply reaching for the stars, but I didn't fancy Arthur Cox on his own. Arthur was a good bloke, an excellent manager, and I liked him a lot. But I wanted Kevin Keegan's glamour and pizzazz, too. It was a tantalising prospect in May 1984, and I did my best to pull both him and Keegan to the Baseball Ground from Newcastle United because I knew they were very close.

Keegan was winding down his playing career at St James' Park and my mind raced back to Brian Clough signing Dave Mackay in 1968, before I had even joined the club, to make a dramatic swansong and a huge impact in a promotion season. Cox was the key to Kevin coming, and after he was on board I spoke to Kevin several times. "Maybe we'll talk about it," he said. "Let's see how things go first with Arthur." The idea was that Keegan would play for a year for us, then join the coaching staff, but my powers of persuasion didn't quite work. Instead, a helicopter lifted him off the pitch after his last game for Newcastle and he put down roots in Spain. For Derby, it was a case of what might have been.

Keegan and Cox were two different characters. Keegan wanted the best for himself football-wise and a good time off the pitch, while Cox had the demeanour of a sergeant major. He modelled himself on Bill Shankly. "Laddie, drinking, be careful," I heard him reprimand players. He'd talk about the evils of drink, although I knew he enjoyed a glass or two when I wasn't around.

Arthur tried to portray himself as an international man of mystery with his technique on the telephone. He told me: "I'll ring you on the phone, two rings, then it'll go down, then I'll ring back and it'll be three rings and it's me." I warned Josie what to expect and when our home phone responded just as Cox said it would, she collapsed in a fit of giggles and said: "That will be James Bond for you then, Stuart … or shall I call you M?"

Secrecy was simply Arthur's way. He was a bit of a Jekyll and Hyde character, very much a "do as I say, not as I do" kind of guy. Roy McFarland was fantastic as Arthur's assistant manager, a role that suited him down to the ground.

We had some good players at our less-than-exalted level, thanks in no small part to Cox's knowledge of the lower leagues. Charlie Palmer, Eric Steele, Rob Hindmarch, Kevin Taylor and Paul Richardson all arrived in the summer of 1984, while Floyd Streete, Steve Biggins and Micky Lewis improved the squad before the end of the year. Trevor Christie came later and so, too, did Gary Micklewhite and Geraint Williams. We finished seventh in Division Three, not quite what I'd hoped for, but those last three signings in particular formed a strong nucleus ahead of the 1985-86 campaign. Ian Maxwell predicted at our awards dinner that promotion to the Second Division would follow, and he and his father duly invested in the squad again.

* * * * *

I swelled the coffers with another innovative sponsorship deal which, in terms of personal satisfaction, was up there with the Saab arrangement years earlier. I still got a huge kick out of finding new ways to bring money into the football club, and Derbyshire County Council had long been on my radar. I was desperate to draw them into the Rams family because I knew the Labour leader, David Bookbinder, was an avid Manchester City supporter, home and away, a real football man.

Bookbinder had forgotten more about the game and culture of football than Maxwell would ever know. I recognised Bookbinder's love of football was something that I could perhaps work to my advantage. As ever, I had been trying to work out who next to tap up for money as I continued my bid to create extra revenue for the club, and I thought that David might be able to help. Football hooliganism was a serious problem at the time, and police charges were astronomic in every city. Trouble was that every time I asked them to dig into their coffers, the county council pleaded poverty. On occasions, they did so before I'd asked for anything – to cut me off at the pass.

I've always been a big believer that local councils should do everything they can to support the sports teams in their areas, particularly football clubs. After all, those clubs give communities a profile, a sense of identity, not just in England but globally, so it's only right to my mind that a little something is given back. David's love of football meant that I knew I'd be able to bring him at least to the table to listen to my proposals, and I struck on an idea that would be financially beneficial for the club but, in hard cash, would not cost the council a penny.

"While I know you can't donate cash, David," I told him, "Derbyshire County Council do provide services which we pay for." He was intrigued. "So I wondered if in return for sponsorship and advertising, you'd write off police charges for every home game."

He couldn't give us cash but he could give us a barter, so we worked it out that those police charges, which I considered extortionate, would indeed be written off and in return we'd publicise Derbyshire County Council as one of our main sponsors. It was very inventive.

David loved the idea – and I was the one who could sell it to his members. He appreciated the benefits of our supporters seeing the association between DCC and DCFC. When the deal was completed it was another first in English football. For three years we didn't pay a penny in police charges at the Baseball Ground, the council receiving massive publicity and benefits in return. Once again I had the owners and CEOs of rival clubs pestering me, asking how I'd managed to do the business and create yet another revenue stream for the club. It saved us fortunes before the council kicked up a fuss, queried the relationship, and it ended.

* * * * *

The money we saved enabled us to bring in Mark Wallington, Ross MacLaren, Jeff Chandler, Steve McClaren and Phil Gee that summer to give us a blend of youth and experience. When John Gregory joined from QPR in November there was very much a sense that Derby County were on the up again, and so it proved. We faltered a little towards the end of the season but third spot and the guarantee of promotion came with a game to spare on a Friday night in May when the Baseball Ground was rocking with 21,036 fans inside as Trevor Christie fired home a winning 84th-minute penalty against Rotherham United.

Buoyed by that success, Arthur forecast that Derby would win back-to-back promotions. I managed to secure additional funding, and, credit where it's due, the Maxwell empire stumped up the cash to sign Steve Cross, Mark Lillis, Mel Sage and a young goalkeeper from Mile Oak Rovers, Martin Taylor. Left-back Michael Forsyth, and winger Nigel Callaghan joined during the season. Cox and McFarland duly steered our squad to the title, six points ahead of their nearest rival, thanks in no small part to the goals of Bobby Davison, Micklewhite and Gregory.

On 9 May 1987 – a year to the day after scrambling out of the Third Division – Derby claimed the Second Division championship with three goals in the last ten minutes to see off Plymouth Argyle 4-2, after which the players and management team dropped to their knees and bowed in homage in front of the directors' box, all smiles and laughter. The feeling was mutual. Derby County were back in the top flight. In those three years with Ian Maxwell I'd found him a delight to work with, but with Derby on the up and Oxford United's fortunes on the wane, the dynamic changed. The Us had dropped back down into the Second Division, and Robert Maxwell did not want to be chairman of a Second Division club – an ailing one at that.

THE NAME'S COX, ARTHUR COX

One Sunday in June 1987, I was lunching in Derbyshire when Robert Maxwell rang to tell me that he was joining Derby County – as chairman. Resigning from Oxford, he put his son Kevin in the chair at the Manor Ground, and introduced his daughter, Ghislaine, to the board there. Then he barrelled into Derby, relegating Ian to the role of deputy chairman while I was retained as managing director. Now the fun and games really began. Peter Shilton and Mark Wright soon arrived from Southampton. Suddenly, Derby were signing England internationals.

Despite the increased interference behind the scenes, we secured a respectable 15th-place finish to the 1987-88 campaign – helped in no small measure by the signing in February of Ted 'the Tin Man' McMinn. Maxwell dipped into his pocket, and very probably the Mirror Newspapers pension fund, to finance the £300,000 purchase of the Scot. Cox fancied Ted, who was at Sevilla, having joined them a year earlier from Glasgow Rangers, but Newcastle were also keen to bring him back to England.

His old boss at Ibrox, Jock Wallace, a man Ted idolised, travelled to Spain on behalf of the hierarchy at St James' Park, but Josie and I flew out well in advance and managed to convince McMinn to come to Derby. We actually drove back to Marbella with Jock, after the three of us had seen McMinn, and later Ted told me he wouldn't have come to Derby without me going to Spain personally to make him an offer.

When, in 2004, the BBC conducted a poll that asked football fans to name their cult heroes, Ted McMinn would be voted Derby supporters' second favourite player of all time, behind Igor Stimac.

Asked to provide reasons, one fan wrote of McMinn: "Not for his talent, but his cheeky, impudent way of pushing a ball past a full-back, running into him and getting a free-kick virtually every time. He would then wink at the crowd, a throwback to the days of characters and entertainment." Another was more succinct, writing that he "did things he wasn't capable of".

Goals were hard to come by that first season up and to remedy that, in October 1988 we broke the million-pound barrier for the first time with the signing of Welsh international Dean Saunders from Oxford. Saunders helped shoot the club up to finish fifth in 1988-89.

I expected a little more judicious investment in a very competent side now, maybe another striker to share the burden up front with Saunders, and I told a friend: "You know what, the sky's the limit here."

Normally, fifth place would have meant a UEFA Cup place, but English clubs were still banned from Europe in the wake of the Heysel Stadium tragedy in 1985. It was hugely disappointing for players such as Saunders, Shilton and Wright, and the club – not least because of the increased revenue it would have provided. Forest, Norwich and Spurs also missed out.

I became worried, sensing Maxwell was becoming impatient when the last day of September 1989 almost heralded Arthur Cox's final day at the club. Everything was miserable for us at struggling Aston Villa, where acres of empty terracing provided the backdrop to the only goal of the game by David Platt in front of a subdued crowd of 16,245.

Early that evening, the phone rang at my Longford home, Maxwell snarling down the line. "Why did you lose?" How can you lose to a team so near the bottom? We need someone who can motivate our players. Sack the manager."

"You can't do that," I told him and tried to explain how unlucky we had been. Cap'n Bob was undeterred. "Call a board meeting tomorrow, Sunday, and sack the manager."

I repeated my stance. "You can't do that."

"I can do it and *you* will do it," he roared. "Now get rid of him." It took me some time during the weekend to calm Maxwell down and make him see sense.

We finished 16th in May and the disappointment was magnified during the following campaign as tensions between Maxwell, the club and fans reached fever pitch. Following the abuse levelled at him, and his helicopter-fuelled abandonment of the Baseball Ground during the 2-0 defeat by Arsenal in March 1991 – a week on from that humiliating 7-1 battering at home by Liverpool – under Maxwell's express instructions I was looking for a new buyer for the club. Despite 17 goals from Saunders, there was no escape. Derby were relegated back to Division Two. Instead of Arsenal and Liverpool, we would be entertaining Tranmere and Grimsby in 1991-92.

Now it was time to say farewell to our two most saleable assets and with a heavy heart I picked up the phone to my old friend, Liverpool secretary Peter Robinson, to alert him to the availability of Saunders and Wright. Peter and I had an understanding that if there were any Derby players Liverpool fancied, and vice versa, we each had first refusal. I knew he liked Saunders because Peter had rung me when we signed him from Oxford. "Christ, you moved quick, we were all going for him," he told me. "Do me a favour, when the time comes to sell, make sure you come to me first."

It was the same with Wright: "Look, Kenny Dalglish fancies Mark, don't let him go to Manchester United, don't let him go anywhere else. When you're ready to sell, we want him." It was a gentleman's agreement; that was how we worked.

I always felt we at Derby were like junior partners in a firm, ducking and diving, trying to keep up with the big boys and beat them. They sat there thinking they could just pick players off a tree as and when, but we did deals under the radar, ahead of the competition. Time and again, they came on the phone to me moaning, "Bloody hell, Webby, you've done us again."

We had been doing it for years, ever since Brian Clough and Peter Taylor were here, and we knew what we were doing. We had to behave that way because we were a club with attendances of 30,000 competing with others who could snap their fingers and pull in 50,000.

As chief executive, I always looked ahead. I previously promised Peter Robinson: "When we're ready to sell, you're the man, although we might not be ready just yet." I dangled bait to get him hooked and one week in July saw Liverpool buy a couple of superstars from us, although I made sure they paid the going rate.

Proof of that was the £2.9million for Saunders, an English record fee, and the £2.5million for Wright – a British record for a defender.

Liverpool met our valuations because they were desperate not to get involved in a bidding war with Manchester United or Arsenal. I was pleased to have maximised the club's investments.

Friendship is one thing, business is another, and Peter knew that Liverpool had to meet what we determined was the going rate, otherwise I'd be in contact with Old Trafford or Highbury at the drop of a hat.

He was a colleague, but you're not doing anyone any favours. You're doing your best for the club because you know deep down that a deal has to be done. Whoever their rivals were in the top six, Liverpool wanted a nod and wink from me that we were ready to deal, so they could steal a march. That's how we worked it. Other clubs knew nothing of the agreement. I'd go back to Peter and say, "Look, you've got to get to £Xmillion, we're not selling for anything less." The arrangement worked both ways and given Derby's financial history, it had to be so.

After my mind-numbing High Court experience and the threat of liquidation, I vowed we would never again face financial difficulties on my watch. It was reassuring to know that if we had a problem I could sell an asset and, if the manager was so inclined, get a swap or a loan player as part of the deal. I'd always be telling our manager to keep an eye on Liverpool players, just in case a situation arose where we had to move fast and a deal could be done. I was probably the first chief executive who worked so closely with my manager. "Can we do this? Can we do that? Could this work? Let's try that." Managers didn't always appreciate me on their shoulder, but many times I knew from a commercial standpoint that such a deal made complete sense.

By now, Maxwell had appointed Henry Ansbacher, the merchant bankers, to sell the club, and they put together a glossy, colour brochure as part of their bid to attract prospective buyers. I became part of a consortium looking to buy Derby County, but Maxwell told me that one stipulation of selling the club to us was that Arthur Cox – the man he once ordered me to sack without ceremony – had to go on the board. Clubs could only have one paid director under Football League rules and as I was being paid as managing director-consultant. I would have to step down.

That was fine by me. Maxwell was so high maintenance that my involvement had become much more than that of a mere "consultant" and I had barely been able to dedicate any time to Lonsdale Travel. I had been hell-bent on regaining control of Lonsdale from Maxwell, who bought a 75 per cent holding in the company and dragged his feet over selling it back to me. But as Mr Justice Davies learned, I don't back down easily, and I chipped away at Maxwell until, following months of tense, tough negotiations, he agreed to my offer. Once again I was able to give Lonsdale the attention it needed and, from our headquarters in Derby, we expanded to become one of the top five privately-owned travel firms in the country.

At the time Maxwell wanted out, Lionel Pickering registered an interest, and after the usual round of negotiations via directors and advisors, a deal was done. Lionel got his hands on the club. I was still happy to be involved with Derby County and to remain on the board because I felt that I still had plenty to offer and a significant part to play, be it with advice or financial support when required. I had also been nominated by the Midlands clubs to become their representative and a director of the new Football League, a position that required me to be a club director in order to fulfill that role. But I was seen as a "Maxwell man", certain parties at Derby wanted me out, and so I resigned and spent the next year focusing fully on Lonsdale. I wondered if my long association with Derby County was finally at an end. Yet it was merely a brief hiatus and when Lionel restructured the board,

THE NAME'S COX, ARTHUR COX

making himself chairman, he asked me to return as part of a four-man team that he was determined would restore fixtures against Liverpool, Manchester United and Arsenal, and take Derby County to new glories.

17

Lionel, Jim and Another Promotion

LIONEL PICKERING was a remarkable man, a lifelong Derby County fan who sold his free newspaper empire for £25million in 1989, shelled out £13million to become a major shareholder in the Rams, and sunk another fortune into creating a team that enjoyed a brief golden era. He was also a prime mover and financier in the club leaving the ramshackle old Baseball Ground with all its ghosts and fabulous memories going back generations, tucked away in the backstreets of Derby, for a £28million state-of-the-art stadium at Pride Park with a capacity of 33,000 near the city centre. What was essentially a monochrome, black-and-white era was transformed into Technicolor. Life with Lionel was hair-raising at times, never dull, and reminded me of that childhood poem about the little girl with a curl in the middle of her forehead: "When she was

LIONEL, JIM AND ANOTHER PROMOTION

good, she was very, very good, but when she was bad she was horrid." Derby were reaching for the stars again, and buying a few, but then Sir Alex Ferguson came calling one day years later, and a shadow fell ...

✳ ✳ ✳ ✳ ✳

During my time away from the club, Pickering invested heavily – too heavily for my liking – with players such as Craig Short, Mark Pembridge, Tommy Johnson and Paul Kitson following £1million striker Marco Gabbiadini from Crystal Palace. Excitement and a sense of expectancy, if not misguided entitlement, grew with each new signing as Lionel pumped in the cash – more and more of it.

Although Derby missed out on automatic promotion in 1991-92, a place in the Second Division Play-off Final beckoned when Gabbiadini and Johnson scored in the first 15 minutes of the semi-final at Blackburn. The rest of the first leg was disastrous, Kenny Dalglish's team running out 4-2 winners. Arthur Cox couldn't quite pull it round at home, and the rest, as they say, is history. Rovers went on to beat Leicester at Wembley and three years later, bankrolled by steel magnate Jack Walker, became Premier League champions.

Meanwhile, back in the East Midlands, I was fully involved once more. At the start of the 1992-93 campaign Derby County were firm favourites for promotion, but the expectations weren't matched and we finished eighth, a huge disappointment. You haven't got a cat in hell's chance of making progress, if you suffer ten home League defeats. That failure, and there is no other way of describing it, increased the pressure on us to go up at the next available opportunity to justify Lionel's outlay. A 5-0 opening-day demolition of Sunderland preceded a 1-1 draw with arch-rivals Nottingham Forest at the City Ground, but the results that followed were a very mixed bag.

Things changed in October when Arthur stepped down because of a chronic back condition, and Roy McFarland took charge, steering the club to the Play-off Final. There was heartache ahead of us at Wembley where Roy's boys, despite taking the lead through Johnson – who had scored in both successful legs of the semi-final against Millwall – lost 2-1 to neighbours Leicester.

Maybe he felt he was being taken for a ride, or used simply as a cash cow, but I knew there was disruption ahead when Lionel thumped the table at a board meeting and demanded £6million of his money back. That meant selling prize assets, just as I had before with Dean Saunders and Mark Wright.

As for McFarland, he looked crestfallen, as well he might, arguing: "Selling off the club's silver was like a suicide note in instalments. It was going to make my job untenable."

If it wasn't for bad luck, Roy would have had no luck at all. During the 1994-95 season, Paul Kitson was sold to Newcastle for £2.25million, Mark Pembridge went to Sheffield Wednesday for £900,000 while I managed to bring in a combined £2.9million from Aston Villa for Gary Charles and Tommy Johnson. I hated it when Derby County became a "selling club" and the money wasn't reinvested in quality replacements. We needed to balance the books by reducing the wage bill, however, and I was charged with putting the word out that we were open for business. At Christmas, it was quite clear that Villa's tongues were hanging out for right-back Charles and winger Johnson. Bids of £1.5million

LIONEL, JIM AND ANOTHER PROMOTION

and £750,000 respectively came our way, and Villa thought they were doing us a favour.

Pickering was in no mood to play Santa Claus though, saying: "It's my money that bought these players and I will not have anyone else selling them. If anyone got Johnson for less than £2m they would be pinching him from us. Charles is a classy attacking full-back and would probably command £1.5million. But as a package we could come down a bit."

Early in the new year, Lionel was in Paris with friends, staying at the George V Hotel, just off the Champs-Élysées, when I telephoned to tell him that Doug Ellis, the Villa chairman, was keen to negotiate, and so the transfers were swiftly concluded. Understandably, as manager Roy did not agree with the sale of the two players before an FA Cup third-round tie away at Everton and he let his feelings be known to the press. To the surprise of no one, Derby lost 1-0 at Goodison Park.

With the team out of the running to reach the Play-offs, the tough decision was taken to part company with McFarland. I always felt that Roy was a better number-two than he was a manager, and that he relied too heavily on his achievements as a player.

He had been some player, by the way, and we all wanted Roy to succeed because he'd been a fine servant of the club over many years, but results weren't going his way and, with his contract due to expire, Lionel decided not to renew it.

The chairman told me to compile a shortlist of potential replacements, which was something that quite often took time. Meanwhile we were criticised by a local press always friendly towards McFarland – "What was wrong with Roy?" headlines demanded to know – while permission was sought from other chairmen to speak to their managers. My final list comprised seven names: Martin O'Neill, Ossie Ardiles, Neil Warnock, Brian Horton, Steve Bruce, Mike Walker and Jim Smith.

Bruce was the man we wanted. An inspirational captain at Manchester United, a great leader, he was coming to the end of his playing career. Steve was impressive; he was solid, a very good bloke, and I thought that he had a couple of years left as a player in a lower division. It crossed my mind that he might be a bit of a modern-day Dave Mackay, and I tried to entice him to Derby as player-manager. Steve and his wife, Janet, drove down to Lionel's home at Ednaston Manor. He interviewed brilliantly, and I think both parties were quite taken with each other.

Unfortunately, Sir Alex Ferguson, who had been on holiday, and Martin Edwards put the kibosh on it. Fergie demanded another year out of Bruce on the pitch, and he got it. I look at what Steve has since achieved in management and I know my judgment was vindicated. Years later, I bumped into Janet Bruce again and she was very complimentary. "It was a lovely house you had," she told me. "Have you still got it?" "I wish," I said, "but it was Lionel's." She thought it was mine because I was the one conducting the meeting.

Interviewing managers is a simple process. Ultimately, all you are seeking is a man who can take your club up to the next level. You need to know how solid they are, their vision for a style of football, if they can inspire the players at their disposal. In those days there were no obligatory coaching certificates or badges, you simply wanted to discover if they had that certain "X factor". That said, had Roy McFarland come into the mansion

LIONEL, JIM AND ANOTHER PROMOTION

that afternoon for a pot of tea with Lionel and myself and been interviewed, you would have probably got the same feeling as you did with Steve, but Roy didn't make it in top-flight management and Steve did. That's how fine the line is.

Swindon boss Ossie Ardiles, who went on to Newcastle United, West Bromwich Albion and Tottenham Hotspur, among other clubs, was a nice guy but we knew straight away he wasn't for us. A lovely man to have a cuppa with, but he was never going to light the place up.

Neil Warnock, who became a member of the much-respected 1,000 club, we talked to, but we didn't fancy him either.

The one who fancied himself, and made a good impression, was Brian Horton. I was away for the weekend when I picked up some extremely interesting intelligence regarding an alternative candidate. Meanwhile, Lionel and another director were interviewing Horton. He impressed them so much that when I walked into the Baseball Ground on Monday morning, I was greeted with the news: "Stuart, we're offering Brian the job."

"You can't give it to Brian Horton," I told to a couple of stunned figures.

"Well, we've offered it to him. He has sold us this dream ..."

Brian had recently been sacked by Manchester City, having previously managed Hull and Oxford, and I was adamant: "Well, I don't think he's what we're looking for."

I certainly did know who I thought would be a good fit, because that weekend I had discovered that Jim Smith might be available at the League Managers' Association.

Pickering shouted: "Well, who's going to tell Horton, Stuart?"

"Don't look at me, Mr Chairman."

So Lionel, with a huge sigh and plenty of muttering under his breath, duly made the call, advising Brian that we were still considering options and that we would get back to him in due course.

I later found out that he suspected it was me who had ruined it for him and he was right, clearly a better judge than I had given him credit for. It was nothing personal with Brian, I just didn't think he was strong enough for what we wanted, and I fancied Jim because I knew he was.

Steve Bruce I would have taken the day we interviewed him, he was my number-one choice, but as it happened we couldn't have done better than the Bald Eagle. His CV already boasted four promotions (now equalled by Bruce), so Jim knew what it would take to get Derby back to the Promised Land. He had been sacked by Portsmouth that January after losing key players such as Darren Anderton and Guy Whittingham, and finding no money for adequate replacements at Fratton Park. Roy McFarland, for one, would have sympathised with Jim on that score.

Jim had taken up the post of chief executive at the LMA, pen-pushing, shuffling documents and dealing with administration, but he confided to my old pal, Gordon Milne, that it didn't suit him. He was a fighting-fit 54, itching to return to the coalface of day-to-day management. Our plans at Derby rekindled the fire in his belly, we toasted a deal over a glass of red wine as Jim asked: "When do I start, Stuart?"

Some of the signings he made were inspirational and none more influential than that of Steve McClaren, a former Rams player who was now making his way in the game as a young coach with a growing reputation as a forward-thinking ideas

LIONEL, JIM AND ANOTHER PROMOTION

man. McClaren proved to be light years ahead of a mere "bibs and cones" coach.

Jim had some first-class contacts, and they went out with our backing to bring in some fantastic players – once again stealing a march on our rivals. He moved quickly and discreetly, under the radar and everyone else groaned: "Bloody hell." Nowadays, players tend to be hawked around, and everybody knows who is available. Deals are flagged up in the press weeks, if not months, in advance.

Igor Stimac, a magnificent central defender who oozed class and composure, became a firm favourite among the fans. A Croatia international, we picked him up from Hajduk Split for £1.5million and he made an instant impact, twice, scoring on his debut at Tranmere in a hefty defeat in November and pranging his motor.

Igor was a big hit off the pitch too, and not just in the Lonsdale offices where the girls swooned whenever the charismatic Croat walked in to see me for a chat. He had genuine presence. There is a now restaurant at the iPro, called Igor's.

What a character. The day he signed, a picture of Igor on the front page of the *Derby Evening Telegraph* showed him being handed the keys to his new club car. On page three there was another story about Igor and the car … he'd crashed it on his way home after driving on the right-hand side of the road. I went to the training ground in those early days to check whether he and his family were happy and settling in, but I missed him a few times because as soon as training was over, he was off like a shot to look at houses. That reassured me that Igor was keen to put down roots in Derby.

He loved the cinema, it was how he practised his English. Igor headed to a multiplex most afternoons to watch a couple of films. The subject matter did not bother him unduly, he wanted to improve his grasp of the language and it didn't take him long to smile when greeted with an "Ey up, mi duck" in broad Derbyshire dialect.

Robin van der Laan was another new recruit that season, brought in from Port Vale, while goalkeeper Russell Hoult's loan move from Leicester became permanent, Darryl Powell joined from Portsmouth and Ronnie Willems from FC Zurich. Chris Powell made the move from Southend in January for £750,000, Ashley Ward arrived from Norwich, and Matt Carbon from Lincoln. Gary Rowett and Dean Yeates had been inherited by Jim.

That 5-1 thrashing at Tranmere was the last time we were beaten for 20 matches, and the run Derby put together – including 13 wins – saw us climb to the top of the table. Sunderland stayed with us, though, and when they beat us 3-0 at Roker Park they went above us. Second place was enough for automatic promotion, to avoid the dreaded Play-offs, and we secured it on Sunday, 28 April with a 2-1 victory over Crystal Palace. What an afternoon that was, one hell of a day. Palace had promotion ambitions of their own and would have leapfrogged us had they won. The TV cameras were there, the tension unbearable, but we did it, 2-1 – Van der Laan's header separating the two sides.

Around the time I brought Jim to Derby from the LMA, I made another recommendation to the chairman. We needed a commercial manager, and I thought that Keith Loring, the man doing deals on Brentford's behalf, would fit the bill admirably.

LIONEL, JIM AND ANOTHER PROMOTION

I was on the Football League board of directors and had met Keith on a couple of committees. He had impressed me. I duly introduced Keith to Lionel at Lionel's pub, the Yew Tree Inn & Lodge at Ednaston, and left them to it. That meeting was so successful that Loring was immediately installed as chief executive and he worked very well with Jim, throwing himself into the job. I was relieved to be able to concentrate on being a director, and I must say I didn't miss the hugely time-consuming, daily hands-on involvement of running a football club. I'd been there, done it and bought the T-shirt.

The fact that Lionel and Jim were enjoying a very good relationship also made life easier. With great tact, Jim would listen to Lionel extolling the virtues of attacking football, and as Lionel noted later: "He listened, smiled encouragingly, made the right noises and then did it his way." To get what he wanted, the manager could play Lionel like a fiddle. Jim met him at the Yew Tree, between Derby and Ashbourne, because Lionel rarely went to the Baseball Ground, save for matches and the occasional board meeting. That suited Jim perfectly as the pub was on his way home. If serious discussion was on the agenda, then Jim drove to Lionel's house, but otherwise it was the pub, and always between 6pm and 8pm, when the chairman had downed a couple of looseners.

The chairman always started with a glass of orange juice, perched on the bar in full show, to prove, I think, to me or anyone else who was around that he wasn't an alcoholic. Jim loved a drink as well, always a gin and tonic early doors, then he moved on to the red wine. He could handle it, though, and he knew what he was doing. He'd been around for more than 1,000 Football

League games, flattering plenty of chairmen. He soon worked out that, with a couple more drinks inside him, Lionel became belligerent. At 8pm, Jim would look at his watch and be on his way. "Training in the morning, Mr Chairman. Must be bright and early. Oh, don't forget: I'd like that new striker."

It was some business the pair of them did in the Yew Tree in those days, too, and more fantastic signings to thrill the fans followed as Derby County prepared for the 1996-97 season and life in the Premier League. Aljosa 'Ace' Asanovic arrived on the recommendation of Stimac, with whom he had played for Split and Croatia. He was a good player was Ace, but the big boys quickly sussed him out, one or two getting stuck into him in the belief that he lacked bottle and could be discouraged. Asanovic was wonderful on the ball, drilling low, trademark surgically-precise passes, and to begin with, everyone was enamoured with him. "Who the bloody hell is this?" But he was injury-prone and made less than 40 appearances for the club. That said, fans still fondly remember the impact he made.

I was in a state of some trepidation when we travelled to Old Trafford on 5 April. We had lost our previous three away games, 4-2 at Leicester, 6-1 at Middlesbrough and 1-0 at Everton, while Manchester United, the champions, had only previously lost three home games in the top-flight since 1992. Oh, and Jim Smith had decided the time was right to give a debut to a 21-year-old, 6ft 4in, Costa Rican former basketball scholar who had been rejected after a trial by QPR. No worries here then, I thought, uttering a silent prayer at 3pm. Thirty-five minutes later, something quite remarkable happened: Paulo Wanchope embarked on a mazy dribble from his own half which left four

LIONEL, JIM AND ANOTHER PROMOTION

United defenders trailing in his wake before he slotted the ball past Peter Schmeichel for a goal voted the best in Derby County's history as part of the club's 125th anniversary celebrations.

It would have been a travesty of justice had Wanchope's world-class effort not been rewarded with the win bonus he duly pocketed following our 3-2 victory to take the most prized scalp in English football. Goalkeeper Mart Poom also made his Rams debut that day. And we might have made bigger headlines for our win at Old Trafford, but on the same afternoon the Grand National was postponed following an IRA bomb threat. With Wanchope on board, Jim led Derby to 12th place as the curtain came down for the last time on the Baseball Ground, on an emotional afternoon against Arsenal. Even the Gunners' 3-1 win didn't spoil the party.

Before the start of the 1997-98 season, Jim pulled a couple of Italian crackers out of the bag: Stefano Eranio and Francesco Baiano. Eranio had spent five seasons with AC Milan and won 20 caps for Italy. After he flew in from Milan, we took him to Breadsall Priory to do the deal, and just as we got there it started pouring down, freezing rain rapidly turning to unseasonal sleet. I caught him hesitating momentarily, looking out the window thinking: "What am I doing here?" But he was a sensible boy, Eranio, very professional and a right-sided midfielder of the highest calibre.

Speculation about Roberto Baggio, the Milan and Italy legend, was rife. Certainly his agent was probing, telling us he wanted to come to Derby. Sceptics thought it was a clever tactic to drive up season-ticket sales, leaking the notion that Baggio wanted to join his big mate Eranio in the East Midlands. We followed it up but

I thought it was highly improbable and, of course, at the Milan end they had got other things to talk about. "We'll come back to you," was the gist of the response. I was fobbed off. Both Milan and his people were trying to get him a better deal elsewhere and he signed for Bologna that summer, and Inter Milan a year later.

Baiano, a pocket-sized forward, could not have been blamed had he put out a contract on the chairman, rather than signed for us from Fiorentina, because Lionel was unbelievably rude when he and his agent arrived to finalise terms at the Yew Tree. Baiano was a small guy, and he came in with his agent who was also about five-foot nothing yet dressed in a tight-fitting long black leather coat. Lionel said loudly: "Who the fuck are these two then? Are they jockeys?" Our guests smiled nervously. They didn't understand English very well, which was just as well, and I translated Lionel's insults into something acceptable, although his manner probably left the Italians in little doubt.

Lionel could be cutting like that, a nasty drunk. Hence the reason Jim knew to get to him before the halves of bitter and whisky-chasers kicked in with a vengeance. I sometimes went in to see him after Jim had gone, between 8pm and 9pm, and it was not a pretty sight. Lionel would stay in the Yew Tree until closing time, then go home to Ednaston Manor and put on old, black-and-white war films. Eventually, he would retire in the early hours of the morning.

Still, for all the hard work and money he had pumped into the club, the chairman deserved his moments in the sun, and there was no one prouder than Lionel Pickering when Derby County moved into Pride Park for 1997-98, kicking off with a pre-season friendly against Italian giants, Sampdoria. I fought extremely

LIONEL, JIM AND ANOTHER PROMOTION

hard to try to incorporate "Baseball Ground" into the name at the new stadium, only to be overruled, much to my annoyance. Those words will always be synonymous with the club. Dumping them seemed like sacrilege to me, although I would have blown a gasket had we taken the old name with us and subsequently lost it to a sponsor's name. Whatever it is called, though, it is a great stadium, one we opened with an official ceremony in July 1997 when Her Majesty the Queen gave the royal seal of approval to Pride Park. I always felt there was a little payback for the time we helped during a royal visit to the Middle East when we played a couple of exhibition games there during Dave Mackay's days at the Rams' manager.

Moving to a new stadium was a no-brainer. Back in the "good old days" the Baseball Ground had been big enough for our needs, accommodating 35,000 regularly – and even a record 41,826 when Tottenham Hotspur, Jimmy Greaves and all, were seen off 5-0 in September 1969. But after Hillsborough the football world changed rapidly. Terraces became a dirty word, and the move towards all-seater grounds inevitable.

Alterations to the Baseball Ground had cost the club a fortune. Adding seating at the expense of standing areas had meant slashing capacity, and the full-house crowd for that last first-team game numbered only 18,287. While Pride Park – the iPro – is a fine stadium, one day I hope they have to increase the capacity by adding another tier with the club firmly established in the Premier League.

One more victory in the spring of 1998 and Derby would have finished in one of the UEFA Cup places, instead of ninth, but it was a highly satisfactory campaign nonetheless. Twelve months later we were in eighth place, and at face value still a club on the rise. But in February 1999, Derby County had been fatally wounded by Manchester United's top gun. Sir Alex Ferguson and his long-serving assistant Brian Kidd had a bitter falling-out over the merits of Dwight Yorke. There was only going to be one winner in that dispute and Kidd packed his bags and left to manage Blackburn. As shrewd as they come, Fergie narrowed down his search for a new right-hand man to Preston manager David Moyes and our highly valued first-team coach Steve McClaren. He chose Steve.

However much compensation the club received from United, it could never be enough. Not that Steve was complaining as he settled in at Old Trafford, winning the treble in his first few months there. But without McClaren's smiling face, constant encouragement and tactical savvy, the Bald Eagle wasn't quite the same, and neither were the team. Steve put a spring in Jim's step, kept him young, but now he appeared to age. In hindsight, Lionel could have done much worse than ask Jim to move upstairs as director of football and given Steve his first job as a manager in his own right. Some at Derby needed little persuading that McClaren had grown to be the power behind the throne.

Derby were down to 16th in 1999-2000, then 17th in 2000-01, saved one week before the day of reckoning when, against all the odds, Malcolm Christie came up with a priceless winner at United, who already had yet another title in the bag. The relegation trapdoor was drawing ever closer. In October 2001, with only five points on the board from seven matches, Lionel cried: "Enough!" He brought in former Derby star Colin Todd to work with Jim. Although Smith and Todd were very close, having

LIONEL, JIM AND ANOTHER PROMOTION

worked together at Birmingham, Jim was miffed. Lionel thought that Toddy should get the job, and that Jim should move upstairs. He still wanted him to be involved at senior management level, to use his experience, but when Jim went down to the training ground one morning, Toddy told him: "I don't really want you here, Jim."

It got messy now and Jim resigned. He thought he'd still be around as an advisor to Lionel and the board, but Toddy felt threatened, as many do in a situation like that. By January 2002, Todd was gone too, and another former player, John Gregory, came in as manager but was unable to stave off relegation. It was a heartbreaking time for Lionel and everyone associated with the club. I now witnessed events unfold from afar, having stepped down from the board and relocated with Josie to southern Spain while the Lonsdale Travel Group was in the process of changing hands.

I was out of Derby County for the final time, and Barrie Eccleston, former head of BBC Sport in the Midlands and Radio Derby, paid me this tribute:

> *I was fortunate enough as the BBC man in the middle of the action as the Rams made footballing history in the early 70s. Stuart Webb was brought to the club by Brian Clough to sort out the administration following a heavy fine and a European ban. He came over as his own man, despite Brian's attempts at off-the-field dominance, and was soon showing his entrepreneurial skills by sealing a global sponsorship deal with Swedish Motor giants Saab, the forerunner of links between major corporations and football.*

CLOUGH, MAXWELL & ME

In the chaotic days following the resignations of Brian Clough and Peter Taylor, Stuart held the ship together and smoothed away the troubles by bringing in former Rams hero and captain Dave Mackay as manager to end the players' mutiny, paving the way for another League championship for the Rams in 1975. More was to follow as Stuart staved off disaster against all odds with a last-minute appeal, literally, in the High Court.

From a journalist's point of view, it was the most riveting time of my career. For Stuart, he could never have visualised when he answered Brian's call for assistance what exactly he was letting himself in for. After a distinguished career spanning many years he left with the gratitude of thousands of supporters and will always be remembered as The Man Who Saved The Rams.

* * * * *

Meanwhile, Lonsdale had numerous admirers, and I decided to plan for my retirement by moving offshore before the sale went through to Capita PLC, a large public company based in London with a powerful presence in the City and boasting many Government contracts. I was happy with the Capita offer – but perhaps I should have held my horses! A rival bid was tabled via Robert Maxwell's son Kevin on behalf of his sister Christine, who was based in Los Angeles. The offer comprised cash and a considerable number of shares in a new, up and coming media/film/technology company.

Uncomfortable with the amount of shares on offer, I considered the deal to be too risky. I should have been braver, for that

LIONEL, JIM AND ANOTHER PROMOTION

company became ... Netflix. Christine was the creator and co-founder of Magellan, one of the first professional online search/reference guides for Internet content, and she was on a roll, seeking a travel content to develop her empire. What might have been!

Meanwhile, Lionel's world was in tatters, and in October 2003 Derby County Ltd went into liquidation. He was majority shareholder and experienced the nightmare scenario of seeing a new three-man board effectively buy him out for £3 – it wouldn't have bought him a couple of pints at the Yew Tree. Three years later he was dead.

Lionel took personal criticism particularly badly and did not endear himself to supporters in an outburst on BBC Radio Derby, challenging one critic: "If you can do better, where's your money? And if you don't like it, go and watch Forest."

Lionel had been an incredible businessman, but he never quite grasped football, never knew how to run the club properly. He backed Jim – which was good – and he did put in a lot of money and endeavour, also developing the club's academy for young players at Oakwood.

But in essence, he always remained a fan. A fan with a spare £10million, of course – and sometimes they are the best sort. Unfortunately for Lionel, in the end there was nothing left. He put a fortune into Derby County and lost the lot. He let it drift and finished up a broken man with a broken club. It was such a shame. Lionel was a keen supporter, but too easily influenced by others. He listened to anyone he met in the pub, particularly his last drinking partner of the evening, then he'd go home and act on it the following day.

Lionel's family asked me to deliver a eulogy at his funeral service at Derby Cathedral. I followed Di, his loyal and faithful personal assistant, into the pulpit. She had said a few loving words on behalf of the family when, to my surprise, I was confronted by a half glass of bitter on the shelf, hidden from view. Not that Di was a drinker, but half of bitter was Lionel's favourite tipple. As she finished her tribute she raised the glass for everyone in the congregation to see, and proclaimed: "Cheers, Lionel." It was a lovely touch and a moving moment. And typical Lionel: the wake had started early!

18

My All Star Rams Team

OVER THE years I was privileged to watch the biggest names in football work their magic at the Baseball Ground. Denis Law, twice, and George Best were both on the scoresheet the first time Manchester United visited Derby during my time at the club – a thrilling 4-4 draw on Boxing Day 1970 – and while the third member of United's Holy Trinity, Bobby Charlton, wasn't in the goals that day, he was always a joy to watch. Bobby Moore, in his later years but still oozing class, was a regular visitor with West Ham, as was Kenny Dalglish with Liverpool. And then, of course, there were the heroes of Europe who visited us, such as Eusebio, on that unforgettable night of 25 October 1972 when the Portuguese great and his Benfica teammates were sent packing with a 3-0 defeat in the first leg of our European Cup second-round clash. Like every other Derby County supporter, I looked forward so much to seeing the great man in action that evening in our little corner of the East Midlands. I can still recall the atmosphere of that night and so many others – the noise swirling around that famous old stadium, bouncing off those high-banked stands that were set in tight streets of terrace houses. They really were wonderful days.

For all the famous visitors, however, my fondest memories are of those boys who wore the crisp white shirts of our club. We had some incredible players over the years and whenever I am asked to select my all-time favourite team, I panic; it is an excruciating task because it means leaving out men for whom I had the greatest respect professionally and admired and liked personally.

That isn't to say I haven't got an XI, though, and I'm adamant that, if they were playing today, then my favourite Derby players would still all be plying their trade at the country's top clubs. It is a team that is tough defensively and contains plenty of aggression – and no little flair – in midfield and up front. They all knew their jobs at set-pieces and carried them out with aplomb, and all had a goal or two in them as well. There wasn't one player who couldn't look after himself and, individually and collectively, none were afraid to take the game, and often the fight, to opponents. In fact, the only concern I'd have about my all-time Derby County XI would be the fiery make-up of it – there'd be fisticuffs when it came down to deciding who was going to take the penalties.

* * * * *

While Colin Boulton did brilliantly for Derby over the years, not least in the second leg of that clash with Benfica at the Stadium of Light, and was the only ever-present in two title-winning teams, **Peter Shilton** would be my number-one. Shilts was a magnificent goalkeeper, his record 125 England caps tells you all you need to know about his ability between the posts. But not only that, he was also a very likeable guy – still is – always with a smile on his face. It occasionally slipped when he was having a bit of trouble with a bookmaker — he did like a bet when he was at Derby, and several times he'd wander in and ask me for a loan to pay off a bookie — but that smile would never be missing for long. Once I got him a book deal with Lionel Pickering — not an autobiography but a deal on the books, an advance so he could settle a debt. All part of the service…

My back four would see **Ron Webster** at right-back, **David Nish** at left-back with **Roy McFarland** and **Colin Todd** at the heart of defence. Local lad Ronnie, Belper born and bred, made more than 500 appearances for Derby – he went back to the days of manager Harry Storer – and when he retired in 1977 he had two Football League championship medals, along with the club's Player of the Year award for 1973-74, in his trophy cabinet.

Nishy was light years ahead of his time as a full-back. He was one of the first defenders, if not *the* first defender, I saw attack with such gusto down the flank, and he would deliver crosses with pinpoint accuracy without ever forgetting his responsibilities in his own half. David was the Paolo Maldini of his day.

As for McFarland and Todd, they were equal to "Der Kaiser", the Bayern Munich and Germany legend Franz Beckenbauer, and the AC Milan and Italy great, Franco Baresi, for many the greatest central defenders to have played the game. What did it say about McFarland and Todd that Bobby Moore had misgivings about joining Derby because he wasn't sure that he would fit in with them?

Roy was a tall, elegant player who could head the ball, pass it, tackle and look after himself, and Toddy, apart from being a couple of inches shorter, was the same. They complemented each perfectly and you'd put them in any team today. Colin missed only two games in the 1971-72 title-winning campaign under Brian Clough and was magnificent again, this time alongside Peter Daniel with Roy Mac out injured, when Dave Mackay led us to our second championship triumph.

I'd play three in midfield with **Bruce Rioch**, **Dave Mackay** and **Archie Gemmill** my picks. Bruce was fantastic, an intelligent man and an intelligent player who could do everything. He'd score goals from midfield, he could pass the ball beautifully, and he could be a tenacious, frankly horrible, player when the mood so took him. Bruce was a bit like Graeme Souness was for Liverpool and Glasgow Rangers – he would whack hard into people, then say: "Sorry, ref, I was a bit late," wondering why he didn't get away with it.

Dave was an unbelievable player and man, whose contribution to Derby on and off the field will never be forgotten. He was ready to head back to Scotland to rejoin Hearts – for some reason the Tottenham boss, Bill Nicholson, thought that Dave's best days were behind him – when Cloughie nipped in and signed him. He won the Football Writers' Association Footballer of the Year award in 1969 – sharing it with Manchester City's Tony Book – despite the fact we'd been in the Second Division that season. No wonder Bill later admitted he'd made a mistake in letting Dave go.

The little Scottish terrier that was Archie, who I first met at Preston North End, was a terrific player as well, and few of his peers possessed his ability to dribble. He was so impressive to watch away from home – and even more so back at the Baseball Ground, given the state of that pitch. He was a hugely popular figure with the crowd, not just with me, and his 21 appearances for Derby in Europe, were more than any other player but Toddy, who reached the same number.

While Manchester United had their own terrific trio up front Derby's, as far as I'm concerned, would be made up of **Francis Lee**, **Charlie George** and **Alan Hinton**. Franny always regretted the episode with Norman Hunter at the Baseball Ground in 1975, and I can understand that because he achieved so much for Derby, yet that is still the one moment that most people recall whenever his name is mentioned. Yes, he was as tenacious as they come, but he could play football and score goals as well, and he ended his career with two Football League championship winners' medals, the first with Manchester City, and the second with Derby in his first season at the club following his £100,000 transfer from Maine Road. Franny scored 12 goals in 34 games during his first season with us, making a huge contribution to that title win under Dave Mackay.

I was privileged to see Franny go out in style, on and off the pitch, in April 1976. He decorated his last match in professional football with two late goals a 6-2 romp at Ipswich. On the way home our coach driver, Eric Kitchen, stopped at a little country pub outside Huntingdon after Franny requested the opportunity to "buy the lads one final drink". Director Sydney Bradley said nervously: "Just 20 minutes now, boys," as Franny charged to the bar. Champagne and pints of bitter flowed freely. The landlord thought it was Christmas as Franny ran up a huge tab, not forgetting drinks for all the bemused regulars. Eric himself liked a pint, but sat there stewing with a coffee, while dear old Sydney nursed a small port and lemon between looking at his watch, sighing and looking helplessly up to the pub ceiling. It was well after 11pm that memorable Saturday night before the Baseball Ground came into sight.

Like Franny, Charlie was one of the biggest characters in the game in the Seventies, as swashbuckling on the field as he was off it – which is saying something. He was great fun around the club but, boy, could he play as well. Only the very best score hat-tricks against Real Madrid. The day after Charlie's treble contributed to our 4-1 victory over the Spanish giants, Dave Mackay was quoted in the *Daily Mirror*, saying that the first of them was the "goal of the year". But the platitudes didn't stop there. Asked if the brilliant left-foot drive had been rehearsed, Dave went on: "Yes, rehearsed by a genius. And you need to be one to score a goal like that." A genius? Blimey! When the great Dave Mackay describes someone in such exalted terms it would be foolish for the rest of us to demur.

And then there was Alan, our white-booted wonder and a man I still consider to be a very good friend. Alan arrived at Derby two-and-a-half years before I did, costing the club £30,000 from Nottingham Forest, and while not every Rams fan was immediately won over by him, they certainly were in the end. His ability to cross a football was second to none, better even than Nishy's, those centres of his delivered with military precision. Away from the field there has always been a deep-rooted respect between the two of us that I treasure to this day.

There are so many great names I had to leave out of the above selection, and even slipping in a couple of cheeky substitutes –

Peter Daniel and **Kevin Hector** – I haven't been able to find room for Alan Durban and John O'Hare, players I loved to watch. Peter made a remarkable and unexpected contribution to the 1974-75 championship victory when Roy Mac was out injured, while it would still be a massive understatement to say that the goals that Kevin scored for the club, all 201 of them – only the legendary Steve Bloomer scored more for the Rams – were a major contribution to the many, many victories we enjoyed. No wonder the fans dubbed him "The King".

* * * * *

I would have loved to have been blessed with the ability to play the game like those boys, but even though the administrative side of the game was always my forte I do have some great memories of charity games and the like. Back in the late Seventies, prior to our FA Cup semi-final at Hillsborough, Lord Tom Pendry organised one such game, and I'm pleased to say, even though Dave Mackay and Tommy Docherty were playing, he still remembers my contribution vividly. I'll let him take up the story:

> *I organised a game against Tommy Docherty's team, with one or two stars on both sides, Dave Mackay on ours. I was tripped and went down in the penalty area. My teammates said: 'Well, you're the captain, so you'd better take the penalty.'*
>
> *I brushed myself off and stepped up to take it, and, while it wasn't the best penalty of all time, it was decent enough to be goal-bound. Somehow, though, the goalkeeper managed to tip it on to the bar but when it bounced back out*

I put it in the net. It was a perfectly good goal, but Tommy went berserk at the poor old linesman, and eventually my goal was disallowed. Doc had convinced the officials that the keeper hadn't got a hand to it, that it had hit the bar straight from my boot, so it shouldn't be a goal. I was furious. My most vivid recollection of the whole episode was Stuart Webb, bent double, laughing his head off at the fact that my goal had been chalked off.

But it was all good fun with Lord Tom happy to strut his stuff in front of his local constituents. I was just delighted to take part in such a memorable event, along with all those political and sporting heavyweights. There was Lord Bernard Donaghue, who, among his many other achievements, was head of the Number 10 Policy Unit under Harold Wilson and later Jim Callaghan; John Prescott, a future Deputy Prime Minister; and, of course, Lord Tom, MP for Stalybridge and Hyde, and a fervent Rams fan to boot.

Then there were the football people, true legends of the game. Dave Mackay and Tommy Docherty, who have already been mentioned, but also 1966 World Cup winner, Manchester United's Nobby Stiles, and Mike Summerbee, the great Manchester City star who had chalked up more than 700 appearances in the Football League. Like me, Mike was Preston-born. His father, George, was a full-back with Preston North End, the club I left to come to Derby.

Yes, it was a great day and it still sends a tingle down my spine when I think that I was on the same pitch as those great footballers.

19

Money Ball

I N THE summer of 1999, the Covent Garden Hotel in London's Monmouth Street provided the backdrop for a series of meetings by football's ruling bodies. Usually the Premier League used the five-star Churchill Hotel in Portman Square, but the EPL wanted this particular business done under the press radar. I was on the Football League board at the time and within football I had become a bit of a player politically. Alongside my old friend Jimmy Hill, I'd already helped force the split that had seen the First Division renamed the Championship, and after we had won promotion to the Premiership under Jim Smith in 1996, as Derby's representative at meetings I had been invited to join a few committees as the face of football began to change. The old order was giving way to a new, exciting look.

Jimmy Hill, by the way, was a fantastic, articulate football man who kept above the crackle of the pot, a statesman, a charmer, the sort of man that FIFA could well do with now as they try to sort out the mess they are in. He was a proper guy was Jimmy and very good at what he did. He was great to deal with, to the point, he got on with things and you knew he could and would deliver. He is sorely missed.

One of the committees on which I sat was to have a major bearing on football as we know it. I realised as much as soon as Dave – now Sir Dave – Richards, who had just been elected Premiership chairman, telephoned me to ask if I'd be available. We were looking for a new chief executive of the Premiership. At the Covent Garden that day, along with club chairmen Peter Hill-Wood (Arsenal) and Bryan Richardson (Coventry City), and Jonathan Smith, a headhunter from Spencer Stuart, one of the world's leading global executive search and leadership consulting firms, I interviewed some very impressive candidates, including Ted Croker's son, Andrew. Two in particular stood out. One was a Newcastle United fan from brewing stock up in the North-East. He'd been to public school, Oxford and Cambridge, and in his interview he came across very, very well. The other was a big Bristol City supporter, a referee on the side, and, just like his fellow candidates, he had a hugely impressive CV.

Aged 40, Richard Scudamore had worked his way up to become sales director at Yellow Pages before spending a decade in the newspaper industry, mainly with the Thomson Corporation, where he had been group advertising director. In his last three years with the company, Scudamore acted as senior vice-president in the United States and was responsible for their newspaper division in the southern and eastern states.

He had then spent two successful years at the Football League, where he had been chief executive, and his case for the Premiership job was being pushed by David Sheepshanks, the chairman of Ipswich Town and himself a major player in football circles.

I liked Scudamore and all that he had to say. He was extremely confident and remarkably self-assured. I did think that his appointment was probably already a done deal, and I said as much. We'd spoken to some very good candidates, and I felt that we should have given them more consideration. Eventually, though, we all agreed that Scudamore should get the job. As history has shown, it was quite obviously the correct decision. I don't think that anybody could have made a better fist of things at the Premier League, as it is now known – we'll never know that for sure, of course – but he has done a marvellous job and I, like everyone else, have massive respect for everything he has achieved in making the Premier League what it is today. Not long after Scudamore's appointment I saw him at a meeting. He smiled and told me: "You made a wise choice, Stuart." That smile said he knew that I'd been taking my job seriously and was in no rush, and that there were no hard feelings.

One name not on the list of candidates to be interviewed for the Premiership post was that of my former Derby County colleague, Trevor East, who I had put forward. Like Scudamore, he would have done a terrific job and deserved an interview at the very least.

The television era was really kicking in at the time and with his background he would have been a very good appointment. Whilst he was not an established football administrator, Trevor had worked his way up within Sky Sports and his experience in television, coupled with an intimate knowledge of the workings of a football club and the game itself, to my mind made him the ideal man for the job. Everyone could see how important TV was becoming in the development of the professional game in England and, as we now know, it would change football forever. Back then I don't think that any of us could have predicted quite how big football would become but certainly there was an inkling that, if it was done right, the Premiership would establish itself as the best league in the world, certainly the most lucrative.

That proved to be the case. Because of everything it has become – the most popular and successful – every other national league is looking to innovate in a bid to generate similar revenue streams. Football is constantly evolving. Certainly it is evolving at a far greater pace than it did during the Seventies and Eighties, and I still love being a part of that evolution.

Eight, maybe nine, years ago, the Americans thought I was mad when I was talking to them, raving to them, about football, about soccer, and what it could and should become on their side of the Atlantic. But look at the MLS now. Granted, it's a long way off Europe's top divisions but the influx of stars such as David Beckham, Steven Gerrard, Frank Lampard, Robbie Keane, Ashley Cole, Thierry Henry, Didier Drogba from the Premier League, and Raul, David Villa and Andrea Pirlo from La Liga and Serie A have given its popularity a major boost. The improvement of the US national teams, both men's and women's, has also given the game a lift Stateside and punters in the US, particularly the ever-growing Hispanic communities, can't get enough of it. People also thought I was crazy in creating the Dubai Soccer Challenge out in the Gulf, on behalf of their government, but the teams that I assembled helped to grow it from a position where we had a camel and goats coming to watch us in the desert to two of Europe's biggest teams, AC Milan and Real Madrid, going head-to-head in front of 42,000 fans.

When it comes to the reach of the game or its growth, there are no limits to what it can achieve, although football still has to move with the times to make sure that it does keep progressing. When he first mooted it Scudamore's idea of the so-called "39th game" was laughed out of town, but mark my words – one day it will come in. Just look at the US model, where NFL clubs visit Wembley each year to promote their product. It is another way of selling our game on a global scale, and if the Premier League doesn't do it, then La Liga or the Bundesliga will, and English football will regret allowing a rival European league to claw back some of the advantage it has gained in recent years.

The English game is adored the world over, and the Spanish and Germans cannot for the life of them understand why it's more popular than their leagues when they have arguably the three best club sides in Barcelona, Real Madrid and Bayern Munich, and when Germany are the world champions. But supporters want to see the players, their heroes, in the flesh, and the Premier League recognised that early on. It is why the biennial Asia Cup has been so successful for the league and why more and more clubs are waking up to the idea of embarking on post-season as well as pre-season tours to the US, the Far East and Australasia. They are markets that are there to be tapped, and to stay ahead of Spain and Germany, and French giants Paris Saint-Germain, English clubs need to give those fans the live games they want. Whether it is the League Cup Final, the Community Shield, or a regular Premier League game that is played overseas, we need to find a way to do it.

Fans in England will eventually get used to the occasional game being played abroad, and fans overseas will embrace those fixtures. English supporters have to realise that the money that is generated from worldwide interest is what makes the Premier League the competition it is, and if the money isn't there, then it won't continue to attract the calibre of stars it does, which will be to the detriment of the standard of the game on our shores. The Premier League has to keep moving with the times.

Such is the growing popularity of football on a global scale that I firmly believe that eventually it will take over from all the American sports, although technology will have its part to play in that and will have to come in even more. I'm not talking about technology within the game, such as video replays, but mobile and tablet technology, which will ultimately change the way the game is watched.

It is already growing at a rate of knots and, in time, I'm convinced more people will watch matches on their iPads or smart phones than they do on television.

With the billion-pound contracts he has agreed with television companies both domestically and abroad, Scudamore has certainly played his part in the development of our football and the world game. And when the Silicon Valley boys start weighing in with offers of their own, then the vast sums that have been invested previously will be chicken feed compared to those that will be on offer. Look at the digital rights deal the NFL has just struck with Twitter, for example, $10million for ten games. It won't be long before the Premier League announces another package of games to their broadcast rights aimed solely at the techies.

MONEY BALL

Richard Scudamore deserves his place in history alongside English football's great administrators: Ebenezer Cobb Morley, the FA's first secretary and the man who drafted the Laws of the Game back in 1863, Sir Frederick Wall, Sir Stanley Rous and Ted Croker. Alas, not all those who have held positions of power within our game in recent years have covered themselves in glory. Geoff Thompson OBE, the former chairman of the FA, a vice-president of UEFA and FIFA, was a member of FIFA's executive committee, but didn't see the corruption going on around him. I'd love to sit down with him one day and ask him to give me an answer as to why he didn't realise what his colleagues – the Chuck Blazers, Jack Warners, Jeffrey Webbs and Jerome Valckes of this world – were doing. At least he might have spotted those "hot and cold balls" that Sepp Blatter has told us about. When he replaced Lord Triesmann on the 2018 World Cup bid committee, all those years spent working with UEFA and FIFA were supposed to win us the votes we needed to host the tournament. Yet we were left with egg on our face when England picked up only two votes – and one of those was Geoff's.

20

No Regrets

IT SEEMS a lifetime ago now, the day I walked into the Baseball Ground in the spring of 1970. I had my ups and downs in the game, just as everyone who works in it has had theirs.

To be successful you have to be brave. But it has been very good to me – and still is – and I am sure that, in return, I have been very good to it. I feel that I have played my part in the history of English football, and the global game as well.

When people ask: "What did you do for Derby County?" I tell them: "On my watch the club won the English championship twice, Division Two, Division Three and the FA Charity Shield. I'll show you the medals if you like. Now you show me yours. What did you do for your club?' Rarely do they have an answer.

I may have had my critics but no one can ever take those medals from me nor deny the incredible success that Sam Longson, Brian Clough, Peter Taylor, Dave Mackay, all the players and myself achieved with a provincial club.

NO REGRETS

Yes, the management staff and players were the lads who made sure we did the business on the field, but without the stability I brought behind the scenes they might never have enjoyed the success they did at Derby County. I have always said that a football club needs its chairman, manager and secretary working in harmony, and then the rest will fall into place, and while it wasn't always harmonious between us on a personal level, we did *work* very well together.

Nigel Pearson and his assistant, Chris Powell – I oversaw his signing by Jim Smith – will work to make Derby County a force again. The story of Pearson's former club, Leicester City, in 2015-16 gives hope to every club. With the right backing, the right manager and players, anything can be achieved. Leicester's story reminds me of what we did at Derby under Cloughie, and later Dave Mackay, although unlike the Foxes we didn't have billionaire owners backing us.

The reason Derby have been up and down in recent years is simply because the club hasn't had a solid base for a long, long time, going back to those days in the mid-Seventies, after the board foolishly sacked Mackay

I always wanted more, I didn't like people telling me "No". I wanted to explore every path that was open to me, to us as a club, or to discover new ones. While I was doing that, the club was highly successful.

Those days of working with Brian and Peter, and Sam, were incredible, and what we achieved, I hope, will always be remembered. Brian went on to enjoy incredible success at Nottingham Forest, winning the championship and two European Cups, feats that have now been immortalised in the movie

I Believe In Miracles, and rightly so. But I'd argue that what he, rather we, did along the A52 at Derby deserves to be remembered every bit as much.

When I see Jose Mourinho in full flow these days, he reminds me a great deal of Cloughie. I see the likeness of the two of them. In fact, Mourinho and Arsene Wenger, when they are going at it, remind me a lot of Clough and Don Revie.

As an owner, a chief executive or secretary of a football club, when it comes to recruiting a new manager what you must ask yourself is what sort do you want to work with? Would you sooner have Wenger, a "Steady Eddie" who gets on with things, building a club rather than a team, and rubs along with everybody? Or would you rather have a manager who will have you tearing your hair out, cause you sleepless nights but guarantee instant success? I know which way I'd vote.

I'm still asked, if I could do it all again, would I put my club back in Brian's hands. I tell people that I wouldn't hesitate if I thought I could control him. The trouble is, you couldn't. Like Mourinho, he never created a player through the ranks as Sir Matt Busby and Sir Alex Ferguson did at Manchester United, or as Wenger has done at Arsenal. Clough and Taylor just plucked players out of obscurity; they went and bought them, then bullied and moulded them. They did it at Derby, then at Forest – Kenny Burns was on the football scrapheap until Clough and Taylor brought him in, and all of a sudden he was a star. That's what they were good at, man-management. But there was no real structure. Nothing was really built to last.

Wenger, on the other hand, is my kind of manager. He's not volatile. He's not going to give his chairman headaches. He respects the club's traditions and hierarchy. He's going to let the club grow as a brand rather than just focus solely on the team. I have been a guest of Ken Friar, Arsenal's former managing director who oversaw the club's move from Highbury to the Emirates, a number of times at the new stadium, and have met Wenger on several occasions. He is a gracious and fascinating man.

While his spats with Mourinho remind me of the Clough-Revie rivalry, he is not like the former Leeds United boss on a personal level. Revie once asked me if I'd join him at Elland Road, on the back of the success I had at Derby. He offered me a fortune but I turned him down because, to be honest, he was too intense. I also felt that he was trying to undermine Brian by taking away part of the structure of Derby County Football Club.

When we met on a couple of occasions, with Manny Cussins, I didn't feel happy in his company. He certainly didn't inspire me in the way that Brian did at our initial meeting in the Midland Hotel. When I first met Brian he was great. He could charm the birds from the trees. But Don was never like that. He was stern, really stern. I'd seen those managers before, the Harry Cattericks, and I knew there wouldn't have been many laughs up in Yorkshire. Not until the day Brian walked through the door, anyway, and I'm not sure the laughter that day would have been heartfelt. Ironic more like. I mean, can you imagine me welcoming Cloughie to Leeds?

Back in those days, I was right in the thick of things football-wise and I loved it. The only thing I didn't do in the game was own a club. I suppose that when I brought Robert Maxwell into Derby it was a little bit like being an owner for me because, as chairman, I had so much power, but other than that I have never come close and, unless it had been Derby County or Preston North End, then I don't think I'd have ever been tempted to push the button on a deal. The time has gone for me to own a club now, and I don't ever see myself joining a board again. Not to have full control just wouldn't interest me. You have to have an affiliation with a club, an affinity. You have to be driven, you have to live there, be totally engrossed in it. I could never be an owner like Milan Mandaric, for example, someone who buys one club then sells it and buys another. You have to "live" football clubs, breathe them with every waking breath, and a good many when you're drawing them back at night as well. You have to be committed and enjoy them with all their ups and the downs. You can't be a "butterfly" owner.

I'm pleased to see Derby County back in local ownership after several years' stable management by the American consortium. The club has a magnificent fan base, a wonderful stadium, and now needs strong leadership. Mel Morris certainly has the financial clout to take the Rams into the Premier League and establish them there. I wish them well.

I've expanded my horizons. I love looking at all sorts of business deals and opportunities – if they're in football, great; if not, no problem.

I have a global property portfolio, and with my friend Dasha Epstein, the two-times Tony Award-winning producer, an interest in theatre on Broadway and in the West End. I'm interested in music and together with my good friend Eduardo Martuet, the world famous Venezuelan composer and music director and conductor of the Miami Symphony Orchestra, we are creating musical partnerships between sport and music. The maestro having created a fabulous composition for NBA champions Miami Heat, we are now focusing our energies into musical themes for the 2018 and 2022 FIFA World Cups.

Spending more than half the year in Florida, I've been invited to join Natcom Global as managing partner of their new Sports Division. We are currently in negotiations with La Liga to promote and develop their brand throughout the United States and South America. Having created the Dubai Football Challenge and the Miami Soccer Challenge, I hold the rights to both these exciting tournaments which will prove to be very much of interest in the future with regards to streaming live matches direct to the fans, either via their clubs or by their preferred gaming partners.

Retirement – if that is what you can call it – is good. I manage my time to get my weekly game of golf with friends Jim Smith and John Blount in Spain, or when in Miami, coffee at Indian Creek Golf and Country Club with Don Shuler, the great coach who led the Miami Dolphins to two Super Bowl victories and to the only perfect season in NFL history.

I now get more satisfaction out of doing my own thing than being a corporate person within a structure. In football I was part of a team, but now I own my own destiny and I enjoy that. I loved being in those teams at Preston and Derby. The camaraderie was fantastic and when I hear ex-professionals say they miss the dressing room, I know what they mean.

I still like to watch the Rams whenever I'm in England. When Derby reached the 2014 Championship Play-offs, I flew in for the Wembley Final. Courtesy of the Football League, two tickets in the Royal Box had been left for me on the door, and on my way into the stadium it was nice to realise that Rams fans still recognised me. One supporter put an arm around my shoulder, and said: "Thank you for what you did for the club. I've come from America to be here today." I don't want adulation. I don't need that. I just want to know that I've done a good job — and that was lovely to hear.

When I go to the iPro, and see the statue of Clough and Taylor outside the ground, it makes me proud. I was, for many years, the custodian of the club while those two were working their magic. When I first picked up the baton it was covered in muck, but when I passed it on it was in a good, clean state, together with a collection of trophies in the boardroom. I did what I needed to do in a time of crisis, and the club was always better for it. Along the way I worked with some incredible characters, none bigger than Brian Clough and Robert Maxwell. I didn't attend Maxwell's funeral on the Mount of Olives in Jerusalem, but I arranged the flights and hotels for the immediate friends and family who didn't make it on board the private jet. My contribution to his send-off gave me a sense of closure on my relationship with him.

Brian was 69 when he died on 20 September 2004, and I did attend the memorial service for him at Pride Park. I sat next to another great of the game who is sadly no longer with us: Sir Bobby Robson, the man I had initially wanted to replace Cloughie when he left Derby in 1973. I listened to moving eulogies from Martin O'Neill, who played for Brian at Nottingham Forest, and his old friend Geoffrey Boycott. It was one of those cold, wet Derby nights – the like of which I knew so well from our times together… Clough, Maxwell and me.